Mothers & Sons

BY **Jean Lush:**

Emotional Phases of a Woman's Life

BY **Pam Vredevelt:**

Empty Arms

Walking a Thin Line

Surviving the Secret

Women Who Compete

Mothers & Sons

JEAN LUSH
with Pamela Vredevelt

Fleming H. Revell
A Division of Baker Book House Co
Grand Rapids, Michigan 49516

Published by Fleming H. Revell
a division of Baker Book House Company
P.O. Box 6287, Grand Rapids, MI 49516-6287

Printed in the United States of America

First paperback edition 1994.

Library of Congress Cataloging-in-Publication Data

Lush, Jean.
    Mothers and sons.
    Bibliography: p.
    ISBN 0-8007-5503-0
    1. Children of single parents. 2. Mothers and sons. 3. Single mothers. 4. Child rearing—Religious aspects—Christianity. 5. Child development. 6. Boys—Sexual behavior. I. Vredevelt, Pam W., 1955– . II. Title.
HQ777.4.L87   1988
649.'132   88-18210

Contents ⊞

Introduction ▪▪

I had just finished speaking at a conference when she came up for a private word with me. She looked so tired, so defeated.

"Have you ever written anything about raising little boys?" she asked. "I'm all alone, and I'm losing control of my sons. They fight constantly. I grew up in a family of girls and just don't know how to handle boys."

"Has your husband been gone long?" I asked.

"He left about a year ago because he didn't want the responsibility of a family. Things were fine when it was just us, but after the boys were born, he was never quite the same. I don't know how my sons will grow up to be well-adjusted men without a father in the house!"

"Many boys without fathers grow up to be fine men with outstanding qualities. It's harder to raise children alone, but it can be done."

Nearly every time I speak at a conference, I have conversations similar to this one. I've found that most mothers need encouragement and practical tools for parenting. Someone needs to tell them it is possible to shape their unruly boys into men of dignity and strength.

Today, many mothers face the challenge of raising children alone. Some are married to husbands consumed by their jobs; others are single parents, totally responsible for their children's physical and emotional needs.

I am burdened for these women. As a therapist for thirty years, I've worked with scores of mothers, and I've seen the overwhelming hopelessness and battle fatigue that sets in when they feel emotionally whipped by their sons. As a mother of three and grandmother of nine, I'm familiar with the struggles of child rearing. It's one of the toughest jobs in the world.

I know this from personal experience, having raised an energetic, hard-to-control son myself. We were living in Australia at the time. The real fun began when David started walking. He found it thrilling to dump piles of freshly ironed clothes into a bathtub full of hot, soapy water. At fifteen months, he enjoyed pulling off the tablecloth and spilling entire meals onto the floor. He was never a child who hung around Mummy, but was always on the run, as far away from supervision as possible. On one occasion I rescued him in the nick of time from our busy suburban train tracks.

When David was three, he occasionally played with three-year-old Andrea, who lived across the street from us. Andrea was a precious little girl with beautiful long blond ringlets. One afternoon David decided to pretend he was a barber and cut Andrea's ringlets off unevenly. She looked incredibly shaggy when he finished the job. Andrea's mother's anger skyrocketed, and she flew from neighbor to neighbor with her sad story. After that, none of the neighborhood children were allowed anywhere near ours for quite some time.

As a four-year-old, David loved to climb. He learned to climb a vine onto our roof, which had very wide iron gutters used to catch rainwater for drinking and cooking. Somehow, David found large glass beer bottles on the side of the roof just above the gutter. He waited until I was busy with another baby, then climbed onto the roof and proceeded to pelt passing pedestrians with the heavy beer bottles. The next thing I knew, there was a policeman at my door, demanding an explanation. The whispering neighbors said, "Those poor Lushes. What are they going to do with that awful little monster?"

David also had a stubborn love of throwing stones onto the noisy corrugated iron roofs of houses, anywhere he went, which led to further confrontations with our local policemen. He continued to throw stones until he was nine years old, and no amount of "correction" seemed to work. Then one summer he visited my father on the farm. While trying to stone pigeons that were sitting on top of a truck, he missed, shattering the truck's front window. The next day his grandfather made him pick a eucalyptus stick for his own paddling. After he grew up, David told me, "Mom, I was so humiliated that Grandfather had to spank me that I decided never to throw stones again!"

David's constant tantrums left me frazzled. He teased other children unmercifully, always knowing just how to find their weak spots. He told his little sister she was an adopted Aborigine, which was very upsetting to her. He was so convincing that she was afraid to ask me about it, just in case the story were true.

My father would not allow David to visit him at work because David figured out how to toll the school bells for dismissal at my father's school. He did this at the most inopportune times.

The Australian summers were very hot. In the afternoons we all took naps. One day I must have fallen into a deep sleep, because I didn't hear any sounds coming from the children. When I awoke, I noticed the back door was open and David was nowhere to be found. I didn't worry much at first, figuring he was probably with my friend next door.

Suddenly an elderly neighbor appeared at my door. She was one of the few people on our street who had a telephone. (It was wartime, and phones were scarce.) She blurted out, "David is being held by the police in the central office downtown!"

He had become bored and decided to run away to his father, who was in war work at the time. That was the last straw. I felt like a total failure. No matter how hard I tried, I never saw any improvement. I sought out a well-known child psychologist and poured out my frustrations to her. She found many ways to help us. David was so stubborn and strong-minded that she found him an "interesting case," especially since he cooperated so well with her testing program.

There were days when David was growing up that I was so angry with him I put him in his bed, pulled up the high railing, and prayed in tears, "Lord, You can just take him!" I wondered why God had sent me such a difficult and exasperating child.

You should know that David turned out to be a loving Christian husband, father, and medical doctor, despite my doubts that he would ever be well-adjusted. Even during his college years, I was concerned about him. Since he was a little boy in Australia, David had wanted to become a doctor, but when he was in college, we were very poor. David worked very hard to support himself while studying for his bachelor's degree, but I could tell he was losing hope about medical school. I set aside a day to fast and pray for him, asking God to renew David's vision and somehow encourage him.

Three days later, David came bounding through the front door, with a smile on his face. Some graduate students at the university had asked him to join their rugby team. David had learned how to play rugby at a Christian boarding school in England when he was young, and was quite good at the sport. He was exhilarated that these older students training for medical school would ask him, a junior in college, to be on their team. There was one stipulation: He had to keep his grades high.

I could see that God, in a very creative way, was

answering my prayer. This was just what David needed: other young men with a similar vision to surround him and urge him on. After this, David never looked back. His grades improved, and his sights were set on medical school. By the time he was twenty-six, he was a family practitioner, and today he continues to serve people in the state of Washington.

Now I know why God allowed my struggles with David. He was shaping me into a woman who could empathize with struggling young mothers. That is one of the reasons I have written this book.

How can mothers help rambunctious little boys grow up to be well-adjusted adults? What kind of goals should they have for raising their sons? Are there skills mothers can learn that will make child rearing more enjoyable? These are some of the questions we'll answer here.

We'll look at history and uncover some parenting principles used by mothers of world-renowned leaders. We'll look at current research regarding the physical and emotional growth patterns of boys. Warning signs of prehomosexual behavior in little boys will be presented. We'll discuss practical ways mothers can create a healthy home atmosphere and teach their sons to work and compete. We'll present guidelines for instilling self-control, maturity, and morality into a young boy's identity. Tips for keeping quarreling to a minimum and loving "unlovely" stepsons will also be included. Finally, we'll talk about ways the church can help the 10 million single mothers in America raise their sons.

Through the years I have met many mothers who felt powerless with their sons. Proverbs 24:5 (NAS) says, ". . . A man of knowledge increases power." It's my prayer that this book will help mothers grow in knowledge so they'll become more skillful in handling their little boys.

Mothers
& Sons

1

The Mothers Behind Successful Men ___ ■■

Have you ever wished for a peek into the lives of successful men? I have. There is a burning curiosity in me to know what makes them tick. How did they become so outstanding? What were they like as children? What people most influenced their development and success?

The more I research, the more I find prominent men applauding their mothers for planting seeds of success during their childhood. They often admit this was a tough task for "poor old Mom." As young boys, their strong wills were like hard soil, unyielding in the hands of the tiller. Their stubborn rebellion was kept in check with their mothers' blood, sweat, and tears. But in spite of these difficulties, their mothers never quit. They stuck with their job, year after year. They nurtured. They disciplined. They loved. They selflessly sacrificed personal comfort and dedicated themselves to helping their little boys become men of dignity and strength.

I do not mean to imply that a great mother will always produce a worthwhile son. What I am trying to say is that a woman can develop the skills of mothering little boys while raising them. One mother told me recently, "I didn't feel adequate to raise my first son. But now that I have three little boys, I am a bit less scared and more hopeful that they will turn out to be well-adjusted adults." As you'll see from the four stories that follow, an ordinary woman can become a great mother in the process of growing older with her children.

A Widow Named Vera

The temperature was about 100 degrees when we arrived at Sunshine Acres Children's Home, several miles outside Phoenix, Arizona. Before I spoke to Grace Community Church's women's retreat, my hostess asked if I would like to visit an orphanage run by a seventy-five-year-old widow. Hundreds of homeless children, particularly little boys, had been raised by Vera Dingman on this desert ranch. Even though the grounds weren't fenced, not one child had ever tried to run away.

The orphanage consisted of many separate dormitories built from old, secondhand material donated by private sources. Touring the living quarters, I saw dozens of pictures of boys of every size, race, and color you can imagine. This was the only home many of them knew. As an unexpected visitor, I was surprised by the children's tidiness. They did all the caretaking themselves, and their humble rooms were immaculate.

It was all I could do to hold back the tears that afternoon. Though these precious children had nothing materially, they were secure, they enjoyed their new-found brothers and sisters, and they were well trained for life. Their mother, Vera Dingman, had given them not just a shelter, but an authentic Christian home.

I was curious how Vera and her husband managed to successfully raise boys everyone else had given up on. Following my visit, I received a letter from Vera that explained some secrets of their success as parents.

I will try to tell you some of the methods we have used while loving and caring for 918 children during the past 33 years. Most of these youngsters came to us with serious emotional and behavioral problems.

My husband, Jim, and I started taking in homeless and abandoned children when I was forty-three and he was forty-eight. We readily admitted we were not smart enough to help children everyone else had given up on, but we firmly believed no child was beyond the reach of God's love.

We have discovered over the years that there is no hard-and-fast rule that works for every child. They are all individuals. So each day we pray for wisdom to know how to help each child in the best possible way.

We have very little quarreling here. I separate any children who don't get along and have them play in different areas. We also try to talk with the children to find out why they were quarreling and help them solve their differences.

Happily married couples help us care for the children and live with them. They set the mood for the home, and it is very important that they be good examples. No one here is allowed to shake, slap, or holler at the children. If the children need to be corrected, it is always done in a very firm but quiet voice. We are consistent with discipline. Children are never told God won't love them if they are bad. We say, "God will always love you. He's hurt when you're bad, and we're hurt, but we still love you."

We have found we must take time to listen to the children when *they want to talk*. It might be at midnight after a very hard day or when we feel too busy to listen, but we must listen. They usually don't want to talk when it's convenient for us.

The worst boy we ever had was rejected at birth by an unmarried seventeen-year-old girl because he was deformed. He was in and out of foster homes and a hospital for ten years. His clubfoot was finally straightened so he could walk. When he was ten, he was admitted to a home for retarded boys, where someone threw a rock at him and put out one of his eyes. He was taken from this home and moved from one foster home to another until he was fourteen. The welfare system asked us to take him because he had become a shoplifter and no foster home wanted him. If we didn't take him, he was going to be sent to reform school. We already had fifty boys at the time and a house full of girls. Jim and I were doing most of the work, washing and cooking for the children. But we decided to try to help this troubled young man.

Jerry did not respond to our love over the next two years. He hated himself and everyone else. He would have nothing to do with any of the other children. He did not like school, complained every day, and didn't even try to do any classwork.

One Saturday when Jerry was sixteen, Jim said he wanted to trim his hair. Jerry was very angry; he loaded his hair with petroleum jelly to make it almost impossible to cut. While Jim was trying to cut his hair, Jerry said every mean, hateful thing he could think of to him. Every time Jerry said something hateful, Jim replied, "God bless you, Jerry." This went on for about ten minutes. Finally Jim started to cry, and he prayed inwardly, "We have this sixteen-year-old boy here, and we have had him for two years. We have never gotten through to him, and we don't know how to help him."

When Jim finished cutting Jerry's hair, he felt strongly impressed to hug Jerry tight. He did, and also kissed him on both cheeks. Jim was still crying when he said, "Jerry, someone should have done this to you a long time ago." Jerry walked out of the room without saying a word.

That day Jerry was completely transformed. That afternoon he began playing games with other children. He never complained about going to school again, and his grades immediately began to improve. We discovered he was not retarded at all. He later told a teacher no one had ever loved him until he came to Sunshine Acres Home. Three years later, he graduated from high school with our youngest son. He now lives nearby and goes to church three times a week. We had the great joy of celebrating Thanksgiving with him this year, and have kept in close touch through the years.

The children we take in have lived with parents who drink, curse, and fight. Here it's peaceful. They get plenty of sleep, the right kind of food, and no one screams or jerks them around. They have devotions each morning and evening. Discipline is done with love, and we cry and pray with them when we correct them. To sum it all up, I want to say that no parent knows in every instance how to handle a child's problems. That's why we must ask for God's wisdom.

A Slave Mother Named Jane

As a teenage slave mother, Jane lived in a one-room log cabin without any coverings on the windows or the dirt floor. Her children didn't have the luxury of sleeping on warm mattresses at night. Piles of rags amidst their master's stored sweet potatoes had to do. During the day, Jane tended her children between her responsibilities as chief cook for a large white family and their slaves. Those she served said she was an affectionate mother to her fatherless children.

I'm sure it was painful for Jane to see her children treated worse than pets in the plantation house. Food was scarce. She and her children were only allowed to eat their master's unwanted leftover scraps. Some days they lived on corn bread, other days, potatoes. It was a rare occasion when they found bits and pieces of meat to nibble.

But this oppressive beginning didn't seem to stifle the development of Jane's son, Booker T. Washington. From his impoverished childhood, he emerged as one of the most remarkable educators, authors, and politicians of his day.

From an early age, Booker had an intense desire to read and write, but as the son of a slave, he was barred from all education. In his early days, Jane saved pennies to buy Booker a spelling book. As the years passed, she knew her son needed more opportunities for learning. Risking her job and shelter, she courageously left the plantation, traveled five hundred miles by foot to a new location, and secured work in the salt mines for slave wages. Near the mines, Booker attended a school for black students while working full-time. Then he heard of an opportunity to pursue advanced studies at the Hampton Institute in Virginia.

Nobody but Jane was sympathetic with Booker's desire to further his education five hundred miles away, because his wages played a substantial part in supporting the family. But Jane challenged her son to move forward, even though this meant longer hours for her in the salt mines and laundering others' clothes to put food on the table.

Very little is known about this slave mother, but her personal sacrifices and unswerving commitment to her son's dreams helped make him a great leader. Washington put it this way: "In all my efforts to read, my mother shared my ambitions and aided me in every possible way. Though she was totally ignorant in terms of book knowledge, she had a large fund of good hard common sense which seemed to enable her to meet and master every situation. If I have done anything in life worth attention, I feel sure that I inherited the disposition to do so from my mother."[1]

On October 16, 1901, Booker T. Washington was crowned with success. "The White House Social Calendar," a regular column in Washington, D.C.'s, newspapers, reported: "Booker T. Washington dined with President Roosevelt."[2]

Booker T. Washington became known as the most powerful black American of his time. His nod or frown could determine the careers of blacks in politics, education, and business. Behind the scenes was a mother who served that her son might achieve.

Jennie Churchill

In 1908 she was known as the most influential Anglo-Saxon woman in the world, but her greatest accomplishment was shaping the life of her son, Winston Churchill.

Jennie was married to Lord Randolph Churchill, a powerful leader in the House of Commons, but Lord Randolph was gone on business most of the time. When he was home, he was cold to Winston, showed little faith in him, and didn't respond to his needs. Some authorities say that no father at all is preferable to a bad father, because then the child is emotionally free to identify with other fathers. Unfortunately Winston didn't have that luxury. Jenny had to fill the gap for young Winston with a rare blend of affection, attentiveness, and a heavy hand.

On one occasion Winston pleaded with his dad to come to a school performance, but Randolph never bothered. Even though Jenny begged her husband to give Winston some attention, he completely ignored her requests. Later in life, Churchill spoke of his father: "He wouldn't listen to me or consider anything I said. There was no companionship with him even though I tried so hard so often. . . ."[3]

Family members complained about Winston's beastly behavior. His grandmother called him a "naughty sandy-haired little bulldog."[4] His teachers saw him as both backward and precocious. Although he read books beyond his years, he was at the bottom of his class in academic performance. His teachers were unable to make him learn anything that bored him. One educator called him the naughtiest small boy in the world and complained he had little ambition, terrible conduct, and was constantly late to class. Winston's headmaster at boarding school wrote Jenny, "Your son is forgetful, careless, unpunctual, and irregular in every way. Please speak gravely to him. . . . I really don't know what to do about him."[5]

Even his own peers were stunned by his antics. Children were shocked at a party when Winston, who had kept adults waiting for him, said, "Everything and everybody waits for me."[6]

I respect Jennie for having the courage to live according to her convictions. She stayed with Lord Randolph, even though she received little from the marriage. Jennie was a woman of principle, in marriage and motherhood. She believed children should be given as much responsibility as they could handle. When Winston was eleven, he wanted to take his mother and friends boating on the river near their country home. Although he had never done this before, he took complete command of the outing. Jennie let him do everything, without interfering or making suggestions.

Even though Jennie had a very active life in politics, Winston knew he could talk with his mother anytime. When he was away at boarding school, Jennie visited regularly and brought him home for weekend retreats. When England celebrated Queen Victoria's Jubilee in 1887, Winston begged Jennie to take him with her to London for the festivities. I can imagine what a nuisance this mischievous boy must have been to his famous mother. When they went to London, Winston met Buffalo Bill, saw the Queen, and sailed on the royal yacht with the Prince of Wales. He ended this holiday by writing an apology to his mother for his ghastly behavior and insubordinate attitudes.

Jennie never overlooked Winston's poor school performance. She didn't take the easy way out and ignore the teachers' reports, hoping he would someday change. One summer she made him study with a tutor throughout his entire holiday.

During his recovery from a serious accident, Jennie took Winston to his grandmother's London home. It turned out to be a happy time, during which she gave him solicitous attention and kept his mind active through the excitement of parliamentary politics. Statesmen of commanding intellect were invited for dinner, and young Winston listened in awe as they discussed controversial issues of the day. Among the guests were three future prime ministers. Jennie encouraged Winston not only to listen, but also to question and argue politely. His mother explained political maneuvers to him and accompanied him to debates in the House of Commons. When asked if he ever discussed politics with his father, Churchill replied, "I've tried to, but he treats me with contempt and won't answer. I've tried to like him, but he won't let me. He treats me as if I am a fool and barks at me whenever I question him. I owe everything to my mother and nothing to my father."[7]

During his career, Jennie sent Winston books that molded his style of writing and speech. She used her enormous influence to get him transferred from one war to another, secured his early assignments as a war correspondent, and acted as his agent for his first stories and books. She campaigned alongside Winston in his early elections and opened doors to all the important people of his time. Most importantly, she gave him her courage and stamina.

It took tremendous energy to raise Winston Churchill. Relatives saw him as a pesky nuisance. His teachers wailed that he was a failure. But Jennie perceived his uniqueness and special needs, and, rather than making him fit into a prescribed mold, she nurtured his personal interests.

His father despised him, but Jenny played the roles of both mother and father and surrounded her son with unconditional, patient love. In doing so, she helped save the civilized world from being destroyed during the Second World War.

Susannah Wesley

Susannah Wesley's life was extraordinary. After being raised in a cultured, well-educated family of noble ancestry, Susannah married the Reverend Samuel Wesley and became a preacher's wife. For thirty-nine years they lived in Epworth, Lincolnshire, surrounded by the dreary wet fenlands.

Samuel and Susannah had been appointed to one of the most difficult locations in England. Criminals who had escaped justice lived off the marshlands surrounding the Wesley home and terrorized the family. Numerous times, the local fenland folk brutally threatened to destroy the Wesleys' lives and possessions. Though former clergymen had been driven out of the Epworth parsonage by the bandits, the Wesleys chose to stay, and, in the midst of this chaos, Mrs. Wesley gave birth to nineteen children, including two sets of twins.

Was it Samuel who enabled his family to rise above these hardships for thirty-nine years? No. History tells us that the head of this large family was an absentee father. From the time they were first married, Samuel made it very clear to Susannah that he would spend little time at home; he was too busy for such things. Most of his days were spent in religious duties in London, leaving Susannah to raise the children alone. This was a woman who intimately knew the meaning of stress! Her answer to it all was: "The best preparation I know for suffering is a regular and exact performance of present duty."[8]

Despite these oppressive circumstances, Susannah produced children of exceptional quality whose love and concern for one another persisted to the end of their lives. Two of her sons, Charles and John, were very powerful men whose influence altered the course of history.

John Wesley awakened England from religious apathy, setting the country on fire with his revolutionary methods of spreading God's love to the unchurched masses. Charles, John's close brother, was a dynamic preacher, but his most important gift to the church was his hymns, such as "Jesus, Lover of My Soul," and "Hark, the Herald Angels Sing," which are still sung throughout the world.

John and Charles began their evangelistic efforts preaching in church buildings, but were ousted when scores of rough people crowded into the sanctuaries to hear the gospel. The emotional outbursts of these unpolished people upset the regular parishioners who were used to a dead, formal service. The brothers moved their meetings outdoors, fully convinced they were called to take the gospel to the masses. Traveling by horseback in difficult weather conditions from one end of England to the other, they ministered to enormous crowds of all economic classes, with great results.

When John died at eighty-seven, 70 million pieces of his printed material were in circulation.[9] Historians say he preached five hundred sermons and traveled five thousand miles each year. Charles wrote more famous hymns than any musician who followed. Their influence on the world was of such magnitude that historians speculate the bloody French Revolution might have spread to England, had the Wesleyan revivals not taken place.[10]

One of the most powerful influences on John and

Charles was their mother. Susannah taught all of her children at home. Today, most mothers have the luxury of choosing how their children will be taught, but Susannah had no options. Schooling was very expensive; if her children were to learn, she had to teach them.

In addition to instructing her children six hours each day, she also ran the parsonage, helped conduct Sunday night church services when her husband was away, and assisted in farming the church lands. Her own passion for learning inspired her children, and three of her sons eventually attended Oxford University. This must have been a colossal task, considering their impoverished state of affairs.

What was her secret? How was she able to handle so many rambunctious children and maintain her sanity? Here are some of the tools she used as a mother:[11]

- Susannah maintained a strict schedule in her home and school, and was orderly and methodical in handling daily activities.
- Her children were taught the importance of confession. When they did something wrong and fully confessed, she did not inflict punishment, but praised them for their honesty.
- She always rewarded obedience.
- When it was necessary to discipline her children, Susannah was mild and kind, but very consistent. She never allowed their crying to manipulate her.
- Loudness was not permitted in the house.
- Respect for one another was a must. None of the children was permitted to invade the property of a brother or sister in the slightest. A pence or farthing (one cent) couldn't be touched if it belonged to someone else.
- All promises made had to be kept.
- Susannah did not allow the children to leave home without permission.
- Weekly conferences were held with each child, and

she treated them according to their individual temper-
aments. Susannah spent two uninterrupted hours
every Thursday evening with John.

- Religious exercises were given to the children morning
and night. Everyone was taught to pray aloud, and the
Lord's Prayer was repeated each morning and
evening.
- All the children attended two church services every
Sunday. Whenever their father was in town, an afternoon session was also held at church. The children
were required to be present. Playtime on Sunday was
a rare commodity.
- The Sabbath was set aside as an honored day.
- The children read scriptures aloud each night. Older
siblings read to the younger, and a great deal of the
evening was spent in singing.
- General family prayers were held every morning.

Today the average parent spends twenty minutes a
week with each child. Most mothers probably wonder
how Susannah had the time to have weekly conferences
with her children and still join them in fun activities. My
guess is that she gave up many self-fulfilling activities to
be with them.

The picture of Susannah's life isn't always pretty. Nine
of her children died in infancy. Most of the time, the
family was cold and hungry, and Susannah was in poor
health. One way she endured these incredible burdens
was to spend two hours in prayer each day. She must not
have slept for years!

Despite her personal greatness, Susannah would never
have been remembered except for the fame of her sons.
Yet today she occupies a place in history's hall of fame as
a successful mother. Though John and Charles, a world-
wide church was born. Of herself, she said: "I am content
to fill a little space if God be glorified."[12]

As I read the stories of Vera, Jane, Jenny, and
Susannah, the skeptical side of me wants to know about

their inconsistencies as mothers. Did they ever lose their tempers? Did they ever violate their rules and routines? History doesn't tell us those details. Reality leads me to think that their biographers have made them out to be supermothers. Undoubtedly they had bad days and made royal mistakes, just like the rest of us. But, whether or not my suspicions are true, the fact remains that they did many things right, and we can learn from their examples.

Thinking It Through

1. Identify something you learned about mothering from Susannah, Jane, Jennie, and Vera.

2. Which of the four mothers can you relate to most? Why?

3. Should mothers offer gifted children more time and attention than other children?

4. If you were able to change one thing about your approach to mothering, what would it be?

5. Give one specific step you will take this week to implement that change.

6. If you were to encourage another mother with something you learned from this chapter, what would you say? Jot down the name of that mother and when you will deliver that encouragement.

2

Normal Developmental Phases ▬ ▪

Elizabeth was extremely exhausted when she came to talk to me about her son, Keith. She had three daughters before Keith was born and was amazed at how different raising a little boy was.

"I had no idea what was in store after Keith was born. When he was about eighteen months old, I remember thinking, *I'll never make it. I can't go through any more of his aggressive outbursts!* I felt totally overwhelmed by him and unable to cope with his behavior."

"But your girls were very active as youngsters. What made Keith so different?" I asked.

She replied, "Keith was much more mischievous and destructive. The girls were curious and pulled things apart, but Keith ripped into things for fun. He was like a whole demolition squad wrapped up in one little body. He liked displaying the power of his body. If he wanted something he couldn't reach, he made a ladder and got to it. He jumped from high places and was constantly sprinting from one end of the house to the other. He moved so fast I hardly knew where he was from one minute to the next."

Almost every mother I've met watches her son grow up with a mixture of strong feelings. When her little boy learns quickly, she is proud of him and proud of herself for producing him. As he delights in his accomplishments and discovers the amazing world around him, she relives pleasant parts of her own childhood. But she is also quick to worry when her son seems too rambunctious and, like Keith, destructive. "What am I doing wrong?" is the prevailing question. Many of the anxieties surrounding the development of little boys can be quieted if the mother understands the normal phases her son will go through as he grows. Understanding what children are like is the first step in learning how to get along with them. Let's look at some of these stages.

The First Year of Life

During the first few months of life, babies listen mostly to what their insides tell them. Many of their sensations are centered in their mouths. This is why experts call the first twelve months of life the oral stage of development.

When an infant gets the message from inside himself that all is well, he is peaceful. When the message is one of hunger, indigestion, or fatigue, he feels wholeheartedly wretched, because there is little to distract him. This is the time a mother needs to form a close relationship with her son and provide warmth, love, and comfort. Having his nutritional and emotional needs met gives a baby a sense of security and safety.

"In the first year, a baby has to depend mainly on the attentiveness, intuition, and helpfulness of adults to get [him] the things that [he] needs and craves. If the adults are too insensitive or indifferent to serve [him . . . he] will become somewhat apathetic or depressed."[1] He may develop tense feelings toward his mother and view her as a source of frustration rather than a nurturer. Spurgeon O. English and Stuart M. Finch, in *Introduction to Psychiatry*, say this may cause difficulties in the developmental phases that follow and lead to an adult who is immature, distrustful, negative, and self-defeating.

The First Few Years of Life

The oral phase of babyhood merges into the anal period of development, which extends from the first year to about the fourth year of a boy's life. Many more demands are made on the little boy now. He is not a tiny infant anymore, and he must learn to yield to new forms of control. Gradually he will learn to control his bladder and bowels. Much of his attention during this phase is centered around the functions of elimination, which is why experts refer to these years as the anal period of development.

During this phase, children tend to become stubborn, obstinate, and even sadistic. They have the capacity to both love and hate another person at the same time. Just watch a group of little boys this age and you will see what I mean. When their mothers try to teach them something or prevent them from grabbing a toy from another child, they scream and demand their own way. They have a hard time making up their minds and act as if everyone bosses them around too much. They often insist on doing things alone and become furious if anyone tries to help. This is a time when little boys resist pressure from others and get frustrated from thinking for themselves.

A parent's role is not easy now, because little boys often challenge the demands of their authority figures. It's important that parents be loving, just, and kind while they train their sons. At the same time, they must also be consistent and firm. The tiny boy must learn to comply and conform to parental demands. Unfortunately, some parents try to knock their sons into shape too early and too quickly. Strong-minded little boys stubbornly and vehemently resist this type of harsh hastening. A strict but kind approach is much more successful when dealing with the emotional needs of this age group.

It's hard to get along with children between two and three. Parents have to be understanding and pray for patience! "Their job is to keep from interfering too much, and to guard against hurrying the child. Let him help dress and undress himself when he has the urge. Start his bath early enough so he has time to dawdle and scrub in the tub. At meals let him feed himself without pressing the issue. When it is time for bed, or for going outdoors or coming in, steer him while conversing about pleasant things. Try to get things done without raising issues. Don't be discouraged. There is smoother sailing ahead."[2] To appreciate your child's development up to age five, you might like to read *Infant and Child in the Culture of Today*, by Arnold Gesell, Francis Ilg and Louise Bates Ames.[3] Dr. Gesell and Ilg studied hundreds of babies and children and can tell you what and why children do things at various ages.

From Four to Six

This phase may last only a few months, but generally it extends for two years. The hostility and stubborn defiance of the anal period gives way to feelings of warmth and tenderness toward parents. Little boys become much more agreeable. I should mention, however, that there is a partial exception for four-year-olds. Benjamin Spock notes that assertiveness, cockiness, loud talk, and provoking are often common around four and require a firm hand from parents.[4]

From four to six a little boy becomes keenly aware that he is male and that females are quite different. He knows these differences apply to his mother and father, and is curious about issues pertaining to sexuality.

During this stage, the young boy becomes romantically

attached to his mother. Some little boys insist they are going to marry their mothers when they grow up. They will want to sleep in the same bed with Mother, frequently ask to sit on her lap, and touch her. Wanting Mom all to themselves, they get irritated when Dad seems to move in on their claim. At times they secretly wish Father would get lost, and consequently they suffer guilt feelings.

Sometimes small boys find it easier to identify with their mothers than their fathers. Learning to be a male child is demanding. Often fathers or boyfriends of a single mother become impatient and cruel to boys when they don't want to let go of their mother. I have noticed fathers get rough and try to shame their sons into a separation from Mom by calling them sissies or wimps. This doesn't work; it only serves to instill insecurity in the child.

"It complicates life for a boy if his mother is a great deal more permissive and affectionate toward him than his father is. The same is true if she seems to be closer and more sympathetic to her son than she is to her husband. Such attitudes have a tendency to alienate a boy from his father and to make him fearful of him, too."[5]

"Parents can help children through this romantic but jealous stage by gently keeping it clear that the parents belong to each other, that a boy can't ever have his mother to himself, and that the parents realize their boys are mad at them on this account."[6]

I've heard many little boys insist that when they grow up, they will marry their mothers. The behavior is typical and can be responded to with, "Johnny, Daddy and I are married to each other. Someday you'll find a very special girl to marry, and have a family of your own." If little Johnny continues to be rude to either his father or mother because of jealousy, a discussion about politeness is in order.

Some experts speculate that the romantic attachment a boy feels toward his mother is part of his emotional preparation for life as a husband and father. Attachment is normal, but it shouldn't last throughout childhood. By age six or seven, the well-adjusted boy no longer expects to have his mother all to himself. He identifies with being male and takes pride in this. There is a definite switch in his outward behavior toward affection. Near the end of this genital period, he denounces girls and shies away from his mother's kisses. You might see a large poster on the door of his room that says: "We Hate Girls. Girls Beware! Keep Out!" Even if there are no sisters in the family, he wants to tell the world that maleness reigns.

From Six to Eleven

There are many emotional changes that occur in a boy after age six. They become more independent and impatient with their parents, and their peers begin to shape what they say and do.

After the age of six, the former pleasure in romantic daydreaming turns to feelings of revulsion. He begins to squirm when his mother tries to kiss him. This aversion includes children of the opposite sex. He groans during love scenes in movies, and is much happier doing impersonal activities like reading, writing, and arithmetic. Much of his energy is freed for consolidation and learning. A certain amount of his earlier sexual curiosity has been sublimated into learning, and he enjoys putting his attention in this direction.[7]

Even though they deeply love their parents, most little boys this age don't show it. They are cool on the surface. "From their need to be less dependent on their parents, they turn to trusted adults outside the family for ideas and knowledge."[8] If a revered teacher were to tell them the sky was green, many parents would not be able to convince their children otherwise, because their science teacher said it was true.

This is a time in life when little boys become rabble-rousers. They drop the vocabulary their parents gave them and pick up tough talk from their friends. "They may lose some of their table manners, come to meals with dirty hands, slump over the dish, and stuff more in their mouth. They always throw their coat on the floor. They slam doors or leave them open."[9] They leave lights on, and don't do the things parents taught them in earlier years. Shifting to their own age for models of behavior, they declare their rights to be independent.

Many mothers become exasperated when they see these things happening, fearing their children have forgotten everything they once learned. Actually, these *changes* are proof their little boys have learned those things; otherwise, they wouldn't bother to rebel against them. Most mothers agree that boys tend to act like hellions at this age more than girls.

I remember a story a young pediatrician told me about his first counseling case with a nine-year-old boy. The boy entered his office, which was on the fifth floor of a medical building. This doctor had practiced medicine for several years, then decided to further his education by working with a prominent child psychiatrist. This was their conversation that afternoon:

Mark (the child): I don't want to be here! They made me come!
Pediatrician: I'm glad you are here, Mark. You can sit down and talk to me if you like, but you don't have to if you don't want to. There are plenty of toys you can play with instead. (Mark looked a bit bewildered about what to do. The doctor sat quietly and watched him.)
Pediatrician: Mark, you can do anything you want in my office.
Mark: (Looking more puzzled.) You mean I can do anything I feel like doing?

Pediatrician: Yes. Absolutely anything you want to do. (Mark went to the window and looked out. A sudden look of frenzy crossed his face as he watched the people walking on the sidewalk beneath him. One of the windows was open.)

Mark: Do you mean I can do anything?

Pediatrician: Yes, Mark. Anything. (Mark rushed over to a big metal toy truck, seized it, and hurled it through the open window. After the truck crashed down on the heads of the busy crowd below him, he went berserk, throwing all the other toys out the window before the bewildered doctor could stop him. Then he flung himself on the floor in a wild screaming tantrum. The pediatrician, in utter dismay, thought to himself, *What happened? I didn't do anything!*)

That was the problem. The pediatrician did nothing when he needed to do something. He failed to provide structure for Mark, just as Mark's parents did. Mark was an indulged child who was terrified of his own destructive impulses. He didn't want to be overwhelmed by his feelings and was desperate for tight structure, limits, and controls. The session in the office that afternoon would have been completely different if the doctor had said, "Mark, there are rules in my office. There are certain things you can do and certain things you cannot do. I will not let you hurt yourself, me, or anyone else." Rules would have helped Mark feel safe and quieted his fears. With safeguards around him, he could have relaxed and trusted the doctor to help him. The poor pediatrician learned a hard lesson on his first case.

During the latency period, three words are vitally important: structure, limits, and control. A mother must set up a *structure* for her little boy. The *structure* must have *limits,* and the *limits* must be backed by *control.* I cannot overemphasize how important this is for mothers to understand. It's my opinion that many mothers push their little boys to think for themselves and make their own choices too soon, in too many areas. Boys in the latency period must learn to cooperate with several primary institutions: the home, the school, and the church. This means they will obey whether they like it or not, because they are not mature enough to make decisions about their own health, welfare, or safety.

What do I mean by structure? When a house is constructed, the builder must first form the framework to which the rest of the materials are attached. This frame becomes the basic structure of the house.

How does this apply to raising a boy? Moms are in the business of shaping their boys' lives. It's necessary for them to provide a basic structure for their daily routines. Primary concerns are the boy's physical, emotional, and spiritual welfare. Once a structure is formed, we rarely change it because other parts of the home depend on its continuity. Let me give you an example of a structure for little boys.

- Every morning he gets up at a certain time and eats breakfast.
- He goes to school and reports home after school.
- He straightens his room when he gets home from school and then has a snack. There is a certain time for snacks. It doesn't drag out through the afternoon so Mom has many messes to clean.
- Chores and homework may be done before dinner.
- He must eat supper with the family at a designated time.
- Bedtime is always the same (except, of course, for very special occasions).
- He is expected to follow rules of cleanliness and neatness.
- Sunday morning he is required to attend church and Sunday school, whether he feels like it or not.

- He may choose to be involved in other church activities if he desires.

This structural base must be strictly guarded by Mom, and she must not bend to her son's defiance. If her husband is usually absent, the child needs this structure even more. Little boys moan and groan about structure and frequently act out against it, but mothers should not change it to fit the whims of their sons.

Many mothers of boys this age report their sons get tired of attending church and try to find ways to get out of going. Some will even make a nuisance of themselves during a long sermon to embarrass their parents. Believe me! I have taken my grandchildren to church for years, and I know all the tricks in their book. When their grumblings start, I said, "You cannot fight with me over church. You are all going, and I don't care how you feel about it. You will be in God's house this day, and you will not disturb anyone around you." This is what I mean by holding to the *structure*. By the way, these particular grandchildren have given in to the structure, and we now have very few battles over going to church.

The structure in each home will vary, because the needs of each family are different. But there must be some basic structure. This is especially important because structure provides boys with *order and predictability*, which helps them learn self-control. It is vitally important that boys between seven and eleven learn self-control, because after this latency stage they enter all the hormonal upheavals of puberty. If boys haven't learned self-control by then, they are in big trouble.

How Do I Teach My Son Self-Control?

"Are some boys naturally self-controlled? Or is self-control a learned behavior?"

I would answer yes to both questions. Some compulsive boys enjoy having rules from without and rules from within. They may even set rules for themselves in the absence of structure. But most boys need help learning self-control.

When a mother clearly defines the structure she has designed, then she must establish the fact that the structure is not open to frequent negotiation. If there is a pressing need to make a change, Mom retains the right to control all changes. Boys in general will comply with these guidelines if they sense they have no options. This forces them to deal with their feelings, to bring them into alignment, and to obey the limits Mom has set. When Mom remains consistent, her little boy gradually learns to make his negative feelings comply with the guidelines.

When a mother rewards her little boy for doing what he is told, compliance is reinforced. Children want and need to feel good about themselves. Structure gives them many opportunities to receive praise and affirmation. Even though they may fight the controls, they gain great security from these limits.

Once the child complies, obedience follows. A little boy's feelings may not be positive, but that doesn't matter. The real victory for the boy is in making the required outer response whether he feels like it or not. This is the nature of self-control. To live in a civilized world, he must learn to exercise this control until the day he dies.

I want to underline something here. I think it's unreasonable to expect a boy to always obey with a happy smile. Sometimes these expectations make matters worse. Let me tell you a story about Kevin.

Kevin wanted to go to a movie with his friend and begged his mom for permission. After all, the other kids from school were going to be there. His mother refused and said he could not see an undesirable movie. Kevin stomped around the kitchen protesting, "I never get to do anything in this stupid house!" Mom scolded back,

"Young man, you take that look off your face right now, or I'll punish you."

Kevin was furious. He knew a way he could get to the movie without his mother knowing: He would tell his mom he was going to his buddy's house, and then go to the movie from there. As it turned out, Kevin never went to the movie, but he came very close to disobeying out of resentment.

I think Kevin's mother handled the situation unfairly and provoked Kevin to thoughts of outright disobedience. She could have cooled his anger by saying something kind, such as, "I know you are very angry with me, Kevin, but I cannot let you go to the movie. I remember how mad I was with my mom when she was strict. It's okay for you to feel angry, but you will obey, regardless of your feelings." It would have been a good idea to distract Kevin with something else after this discussion, to take the focus off the battle going on inside him.

When a mother sets limits, she must also make sure these limits work. Opportunities for breaking the rules must be restricted. If a son thinks he can maneuver around his mother's mandates, he will. But if he knows she will supervise his coming and going, he is less likely to sneak behind her back. A boy asking permission to spend the day with a friend should be suspected if he has just been denied the right to attend a particular activity. A phone call to his friend's parents or an unexpected appearance from Mom works wonders. A little boy needs to feel his mom has eyes in the back of her head.

The habit of compliance eventually takes hold of a boy when Mom consistently insists on structure, limits, and control. This is hard work for Mom, but the struggles she encounters have a purpose. When a son begins to feel good about the results of compliance, it becomes easier for him to yield. In time he will accept some of these controls and sense the satisfaction and power self-control gives him. If he learns these things during this phase of life, when he gets older, he'll want to please his parents and seek to make their values his own.

There is a story from Europe I love to tell when I'm explaining the necessity of a boy learning limits and control. Once upon a time, there was a little village in Europe that was surrounded by forests. The townfolk were always on the lookout for wild dragons living in the midst of the trees.

One day a villager found a baby dragon on the edge of the woods, helplessly cold and shivering because of the snow in the forest. He looked so little and cute that the humble villager couldn't resist taking him home. He was such a pretty creature. All the children loved him, saying, "He will never grow up to be a bad dragon. He's too cute!"

As the days passed the little dragon ate all the food in sight and grew at a tremendous rate. The more he ate, the more food he demanded. When he didn't get what he wanted, he became very unpleasant, so the villagers always gave him the best of everything.

Before long he learned to breathe fire from his nostrils, and the townfolk were afraid to refuse his demands. When winter came, they had no meat for their families, because the dragon consumed their entire supply. The darling little dragon had turned into a terrifying monster, and all the villagers lived in fear from one day to the next. The story tells us that the monster eventually destroyed every living creature in the little village and then destroyed himself.

Many darling little baby boys turn out to be "dangerous monsters" like this dragon because they are given every-thing they want when they should be structured, limited, and controlled. Some mothers, afraid of their sons' rebel-lious tantrums, shy away from crossing swords with them. The sad part of this is that spoiled little boys are miserably unhappy because nobody likes them in the long run.

But when a mother takes control and doesn't allow her son to act on every selfish impulse, security is bred deep into his character. The truth is, it's frightening for a boy to see his mom weak. He is actually relieved when he senses she is in control.

In this chapter we have reviewed some of the developmental phases of boyhood. It's a wonder that mothers can keep up with their sons during these rapid changes. Transitions seem to happen almost every year for a boy, and this means a mother must change, too. Her son switches from a cuddly little darling one year to a feisty, obstinate rascal the next. Who ever said motherhood was easy?

Thinking It Through

1. Have you found boys are more of a challenge to raise than girls? Why?

2. How do you usually react to your children's mischief? Do you explode, take it in stride, or clam up? What forms of discipline do you use?

3. How are you teaching your children structure, limits, and control?

4. How do you handle your children when they defy your instructions?

5. Do your sons battle with you over going to church? How do you handle this in your home?

6. What do you think about the idea, "It is important for a child to obey, whether he likes it or not?"

7. If you were to encourage another mother with something you learned from this chapter, what would you say? Name that person, and then set a time to deliver the encouragement.

3

The Roller-Coaster Years ■

As a counselor, I am sensitive to the fact that many mothers have difficulty dealing with the vast changes that occur in their little boys between the ages of nine and fourteen. I'd like mothers to know they are not alone. This is a time of life when their sons will experience extreme behavioral and attitudinal changes, as Gesell, Ilg, and Ames explain in their books on child development.

The Needs of a Nine-Year-Old

As a nine-year-old, Sam has become much more independent than he was at eight. His concentration abilities have increased, and he keeps busy most of the time. Practicing skills and performing correctly makes him happy. The key word for Sam at this age is *movement*. He will wrestle with anyone who is around, roll on the floor, and fiddle with everything at his disposal.

One afternoon Sam flung himself down on the couch and rolled off onto the floor over and over again. During momentary pauses in this routine, he picked at his nails, bit them, slid down the easy chair, ran his hand through his hair, and then went back to flopping from the couch to the floor again. This was his way of letting off steam.

Although Sam loves being at home with his family, he detests being babied. He would much rather approach his parents for help than have them come to him. His main traits are realism, self-motivation, and reasonableness. Sam has broadened his horizons and become aware of families and cultures outside his own. Of course, he wants to talk constantly about everything. Poor Mom is apt to get an earful at some of the most inopportune times. But it's necessary that someone attentively listen to Sam's jabber. Many experts concur that nine-year-olds tend to worry more than other children, and they need to share their worries with someone they trust.

When my daughter Heather was nine, she taught me a hard lesson about listening. At the time, Lyall and I were in charge of a large dormitory full of girls, and our family lived in the dorm. One winter night the principal of the school warned me to be on guard around the clock, because he had heard a rumor that some of the younger girls were planning to sneak out of the dorm. I was jittery all evening and watched closely for anything unusual.

I suddenly noticed it was 8:30 P.M., the time I always spent with Heather. We had a bedtime ritual that was very important to her. During the daytime, it was difficult for me to have private time with Heather because I had to "mother" numerous other youngsters as well as my own. So every evening we had our own special time together.

I rushed down to the family room to find Heather. She was unusually slow and quiet that night. I was the opposite, frantically busy and tense. I kept trying to think of a way to settle her into bed in less time than usual.

The minutes ticked by and Heather did not budge from her slow pace despite my direct hints. "I don't have much time tonight, Heather, you will have to hurry." She ignored my words and signals. My feelings began to boil. At last she climbed into bed and asked me to tuck her in. Then she fussed because the covers were not quite straight.

I stood up, hoping to avoid further conversation, my ears alert for any unusual noises coming from the main area of the dormitory. I was about to hurry away when she said, "Mom. Sit down on my bed and talk to me." I sat on the bed, rigid and anxiously poised for flight, still listening for sounds from the dormitory.

"Mommy, I want to talk to you."

"What is it, dear?" I replied.

"I can't talk to you when you are *like that!*"

I tried to relax, and then said, "Come on, dear, what do you want to say to me?" I was hoping there wasn't anything important to discuss, because I needed to get back to the main dormitory.

"Please lie down with me on my bed," Heather said.

"Oh, all right." Heather was absolutely silent after I laid down, and I was getting very impatient. "If you want to tell me something, Heather, go ahead. Tell me about it now."

I'll never forget what she said after that: "Mommy, I can't talk to you the way you are tonight. You must *lie down in your soul first.*"

At that point I threw thoughts of the dormitory out of my head and gave Heather my undivided attention. My body went limp. Heather obviously felt the difference, because after that she unloaded the tremendous burden she had been carrying all day.

"All the kids in class tease me because I lisp. Today the teacher made fun of me by imitating the way I talk in front of the whole class. Then she said I talked like that because I like being a baby."

The tears flowed. Heather had been completely humiliated. Then she cried out, "Why didn't you and Daddy tell me I sounded so awful? Why didn't you do something about it? The teacher said I have a problem." I assured her the problem would be handled the next morning.

I went straight to the principal, who specialized in helping children with speech problems. He gladly gave Heather therapy, and the lisp was quickly corrected.

I learned a big lesson from this incident. Children are very sensitive to the way we respond to them. We cannot fool our kids about the quality of our attentiveness. The moral of this story is that your nine-year-old needs to be heard. And when you listen, lie down in your soul first.

The Terrific Age of Ten

Ten is a delightful age for little boys. They have reached a plateau where they are assimilating, balancing, and consolidating their resources. They are fairly even-tempered and love their parents and family. Some people refer to the tenth year as the golden age of transition, because the wonderful aspects of childhood seem to peak at this time.

Carl is a typical ten-year-old. He is content to stay close to home and feels very close to his family. When I asked him what he thought about politics, he said, "Oh, we are all Democrats at our house. Those others don't know anything about the real people in our country." He frequently quotes his mother and father verbatim and rarely has a conflicting opinion of his own. Carl sees himself as an extension of his family, not as a separate individual.

School is fun for Carl, and it isn't hard for him to comply with his teachers. The firm structure of school gives him a sense of security while he is completing the last years of his latency phase. When I asked him about his teacher, he said, "Everybody loves our teacher, Mr. Anderson, except for a few of the bad kids who are always getting into trouble." Carl was much more rambunctious at eight and nine, but now he doesn't want to be "bad" because he knows this would upset the adults he loves. He seems to be drawn to strong male teachers who insist their students obey the rules. He says, "Classes go better with that kind of teacher."

Like many ten-year-olds, Carl believes in God, but he isn't all that enthused about going to church. Sometimes he takes something to read during the sermon, to help pass the time. Though his parents don't always like this, I can guarantee that people sitting around them are relieved when his parents go along with it.

Carl and all of his ten-year-old buddies love to play. I live on a private road where they ride their bikes nearly every waking minute of the day. Go! Go! Go! They bounce from one activity to the next. Football teams, skateboards, and Little Leagues all play a part in their weekly schedules.

Activity is a must for ten-year-olds. When boys are busy with projects they enjoy, they are much more cooperative with Mom on the home front. If Mom is smart, she will encourage her son to become involved in a reasonable number of hobbies.

Hobbies

I recently visited a hobby and craft show in my grand-child's school and was amazed to see the intense interest the young boys showed in all the displays. It was fun to watch the bargaining that occurred among the boys for comic books and baseball cards. They were deadly serious about their collections!

The hobby show brought back memories of my own son's projects. He loved making airplanes out of paper-thin pieces of wood and globs of glue. Next came the stamp collections. He left little dishes of water all around the house, with torn envelopes soaking in them to loosen the stamps. Eventually, we built a shelf across one end of his room for all his paraphernalia. I must confess that 99 percent of the time it was a royal mess, but the shelf helped keep the clutter off his desk and out of the rest of the house.

I frequently hear ten-year-olds complain about younger brothers and sisters taking their treasured items. If a boy has his own special "space," and this space is off-limits to the rest of the family, chances are that quarreling between siblings will be less frequent. A collection table is also a good idea for a restless ten-year-old who doesn't have any hobbies. If he knows he can make a mess without having to leave things spotless before doing something else, he is likely to try a new project. In the process he will increase his concentration skills, express himself, and broaden his education.

One word of caution. A little boy generally enjoys a variety of hobbies and jumps from one thing to another. One week he may show great interest in a certain item and the next week totally ignore it. Parents are wise not to make premature investments in these projects. We learned that the hard way. After spending many dollars on stamps, we saw the collection permanently shoved aside for other projects.

Eruptions in the Eleventh Year

I feel like a herald with a trumpet sounding a warning: "Mothers, get ready! Your ten-year-old is now eleven. Brace yourselves!"

"What's happened to my little boy? He yells at me when I don't deserve it. He stamps his feet when he's mad. He rushes out of the house banging doors behind him and is an unmerciful tease to his brothers and sisters!" mothers cry.

This is typical behavior for an eleven-year-old. Eleven is an explosive time of life because a boy's latency period is nearly over and the rapid developments of puberty are just ahead. He's on the brink of many drastic physical changes, and his male hormones are beginning to "rev up" production. He has no idea that he's so tempestuous and often wonders why his family complains about his bad attitude. The following are characteristics of an eleven-year-old:

- He is more diversified.
- He is more negative and critical of his mother.
- He challenges everybody and everything. The docile days are over.
- He is more self-assertive and very talkative.
- His outbursts are frequent, loud, and rude.
- He is exuberant and boisterous.
- He moves every part of his body, twisting, bouncing up and down, knocking his knees together, and so forth.
- He is not poised, but blunt.
- He hates chores and is very resistive. Whereas the ten-year-old was much more compliant, the eleven-year-old will say things like, "I don't have to do anything I don't want to do."
- Brenda Carlton, children's director at the Missionary Alliance Church of Seattle, says children from un-churched families are usually more eager to learn in Sunday school than those who have been raised in the church. Many boys this age don't participate very well, but they do sit and listen.

Despite this grim picture, an eleven-year-old boy can be charming, entertaining, and love being with his family. It seems this is an age of contradictions. He needs his mother's affection and the security of knowing she cares, in spite of his antics.

Family gatherings with relatives are fun, and he is drawn to the noisy hubbub of a crowded celebration. Group activities excite him at home and school. Wanting a challenge, he mingles with other boys his age to compete in clubs and games.

I've been amazed watching eleven-year-old boys on bikes chase girls on bicycles in order to tap their front wheels and dash away. They remind me of annoying mosquitoes buzzing about trying to find a target. When the girls get angry at them, the boys are exhilarated and feel superior, saying, "Those girls are so immature. They can't even take a joke."

One afternoon five girls were playing in our wide driveway near the road, and suddenly I heard high squeals coming from them. Eleven-year-old Katy ran inside, yelling, "Nana! Nana! Please make the boys go away. They keep riding their bikes into our little play garden."

"Why don't you tell them to leave?" I replied.

Totally exasperated she cried, "They say they have as much right to play here as we do!"

"Okay, Katy. Try this. Go outside and completely ignore them. Pretend they aren't there. If they can't bug you, they'll go away." Katy went outside and whispered the plan to her girlfriends. Five minutes later the boys left.

Boys this age are not only pests, they are also perpetual movers. They bounce about, they're restless and noisy, and they trip over furniture and clumsily break things. It's quite an experience to watch TV with them. As soon as a commercial starts, they roll off their seats onto the floor, grab at other people's feet, pull over chairs, and wrestle with anything available until their program comes back on. I find myself constantly saying,

"For goodness sake. Can't you boys be still for just a few short minutes?"

Though they love constant activity, they don't like to channel their energies into work. With such high social interests, they despise doing tasks on their own. Experts agree this age is tough on mothers because boys typically fly into sudden outbursts when they're expected to perform duties. But mothers must stand their ground, because backing down teaches boys this age that a display of anger is effective, which is not the desired lesson.[1]

Tamed Down at Twelve

The explosive eleven-year-old gradually turns into a slightly more mellow twelve-year-old. He doesn't tease his brothers and sisters as much, and Mom usually finds her son better natured and more able to control his impulsive outbursts. While the ninth and eleventh years were filled with rip-roaring upheavals, the tenth and twelfth years seem to be a time when boys level out emotionally. They have a keen sense of loyalty. If they know adults who appreciate them, they identify with those adults, are loyal to them, and learn much from them.

Many boys enter puberty at age twelve. Some begin as early as ten, and slower developers start as late as fourteen. A boy this age may suddenly double his growth rate. The penis, testicles, and scrotum all develop rapidly. Pubic hair grows first; hair appears later in the armpits and on the face. With his voice cracking and deepening, this is an age of personal awkwardness as a boy tries to gain control of his new body and feelings. His partial claim to both boyhood and manhood is evident in the ups and downs of his voice.

It's common for twelve-year-olds to complain that their

parents don't allow them enough freedom. I know a number of little twelve-year-old boys who love the adventure of traveling long distances on their bikes, but many families live in areas where such freedom is a thing of the past. I suggest mothers tell them, "I trust your good sense to stay out of harm, but I am concerned about others harming you." Often the twelve-year-old will respond, "I'm old enough to take care of bad people who try to harm me. I've learned self-defense and all that stuff at school."

"It is natural for children nearing adulthood to insist on their rights, and parents need to be reminded that they are changing. But parents don't have to take every claim at its face value. The fact is that adolescents are also scared of growing up."[2] They are insecure about their abilities to master all the changes their age demands. They worry about past mistakes and wonder if they'll be able to handle what life holds in the future. Although their pride hinders them from asking for help, they desperately want guidance from others. Many times I've heard young adolescents say, "I wish my parents would give me some rules, like my friends have."

Overbearing, autocratic parents don't get very far with twelve-year-olds. "Children this age want to discuss differences with their parents in an adult-to-adult fashion. If the argument comes out a draw, though, the parents shouldn't be so scrupulously democratic that they assume the child is as likely to be as right as they are. The parents' experience should be presumed to count for a lot. In the end parents should confidently express their judgment and, if appropriate, explicit requests. They owe their children this clarity and definiteness."[3]

If there is anything that will bristle the hair on the back of a twelve-year-old's neck it's the statement, "You need a baby-sitter." Boys hate to hear this and insist they can manage quite well on their own. But in my opinion, they still need supervision. In order to keep peace in our home, I've told my grandsons, "You must have a supervisor while your mother and I are gone. You are to report your actions and whereabouts at all times to the person who is supervising." Appealing to their quest for liberation, I've said, "Report back to the supervisor each hour," rather than "Mind your baby-sitter." Everyone was much happier when we left on these terms.

From his ninth to his twelfth year, the young boy and his parents experience the ups and downs of growing older together. Many mothers who have already raised their children say life seemed to be more on an even keel during their son's twelfth year. But they'll also tell you to hang on tight and get ready for the whirlwind, hair-raising 365 days just around the corner.

Thinking It Through

1. Has there ever been a time when your children have taught you a lesson about "lying down in your soul"? Explain.

2. Hobbies are important for little boys. What hobbies do your children enjoy?

3. Many mothers report there are major eruptions during their sons' eleventh year. Did you or other mothers you know have problems with your children at that age? Explain.

4. Were those children more tamed down at twelve? What changes did you notice?

5. If you were to encourage another mother with something you learned from this chapter, what would you say? Who will you encourage? When?

4

I'm Going to Throttle My Thirteen-Year-Old! _____ ▪

I was recently talking with a mother of a thirteen-year-old boy. Out of curiosity, I said, "Without thinking much about it, tell me about your son." I had so many good laughs with her over the typical crazy things thirteen-year-olds do that I had to share part of our conversation with you. Without hesitating, she said:

He is just like a premenstrual teenage girl, totally irritable at times, with a trigger-happy temperament. He loves to set me up, too. Last night when I was cooking supper, he said he was ravenous and immediately wanted something to eat. He couldn't possibly wait for supper. As I hurried to get the meal on the table, I tried to distract him by showing him some snapshots that I had enlarged for gifts. In disgust, he turned to me and said, "I don't like them, and your breath stinks." He decided he didn't want to eat, stormed off to his bedroom, and slammed the door.

To be frank, I was very hurt and glad he left the room. I think I could have throttled him. But the strange thing is, just before bedtime he came out of his room and said, "I really do love you very much, Mom," then went back inside and closed the door.

Most of the time his room is a mess. But when he does clean it, he makes a big production out of it and insists I admire his orderliness. Yesterday I "oohed and aahed" over his neatness and a few moments later I found his new clothes strewn all over the floor. When I told him to take care of his belongings because we didn't have the money for more clothes, he said, "That's not my fault. I didn't ask to be born."

I am well acquainted with this little boy, and even though he makes these remarks to his mother, I know he worries very much about unpaid bills and his shabby clothes. Believe it or not, he loves his mother deeply and is fiercely loyal to her when she is not around.

This gives us a picture of the young boy thrust into early adolescence. It's a difficult age. While the twelve-year-old is blithe, the thirteen-year-old is reflective and moody. He's a challenge to understand, because so many new behaviors emerge during this year. Unwilling to communicate openly, he tends to withdraw from his family circle. This marks a big change, because earlier he loved being in the center of family activities. However, when he withdraws, it's not that he's retreating from reality; he just needs to probe more into himself.

This is a frustrating age for mothers, because many boys are in the middle of a fantastic growth spurt. It seems these drastic physical changes go hand in hand with a more lax attitude toward school and hobbies. Now Mom is left with the challenge of playing cheerleader to motivate her son in things he used to do on his own.

A distraught mother of a thirteen-year-old called me recently and said, "I'm shocked. Chuck's school just called to tell me Chuck has been given five pink slips in the last several weeks. I haven't seen any of them. They say he isn't handing in his assignments."

"That's odd. You told me a few weeks ago he was much happier this year at school."

"I thought everything was okay. He constantly tells me he is doing fine in school. Whenever I question him about his homework, he gets huffy and says it's already done."

This particular boy was a chubby, baby-faced kid a little over a year ago. In the last fifteen months, he has become so big and tall, he looks like a full-grown man. The truth is, he is only thirteen. Even though he tests very high academically, it seems he has lost some interest in school during this dramatic growth period.

The boy who's slower in development and still a "shrimp" when his friends look like full-grown men needs reassurance that he will catch up with his buddies in time. There is a vast difference in growth rates at this age. These concerns are very painful for those who lag behind the others, because physique and athletic abilities are important to their peers. They feel they must keep up with the other guys in order to be accepted by them.

A mother worries about her boy's touch-me-not attitude at this age. His radical changes from one emotion to the next make her feel she's been hit by a tornado and left to sit in the dust while her son goes his merry way.

Actually these testy attitudes toward Mom differ greatly from the feelings he has deep inside. He loves his mother but has an instinctive drive to emancipate himself from her. The closer he is to his mother, the more friction there will be as he pulls away from her. Mom is likely to feel hurt and rejected time and again. Just when it seems she is recapturing the closeness they shared when he was small, the thirteen-year-old begins feeling swallowed up by his mother and danger signals flash in front of him. He panics and views his mother as a wicked witch who is slowly destroying his chance to grow into manhood as a separate individual.

When mothers try to grasp for the closeness they had with their sons as little boys, they will be pushed away.

The thirteen-year-old is compelled to create distance between himself and the most powerful female in his life. Perhaps he senses his mother will not separate from him until he causes some distance between them. He doesn't necessarily fight his mother as he would an enemy. Sometimes he simply leaves the safe arena of her love and withdraws into his own little world, where she cannot enter. Each time he maneuvers for his release into manhood, he feels stronger and more secure as a male.

But then comes another big switch. After withdrawing, he feels safe and more secure as an individual and senses he can afford to be a little boy again. Mom suddenly finds her charming "real" son back in the fold. Poor Mom! She tries her best to preserve this closeness with him, free from the ups and downs, but it doesn't work. He will continue this advance-retreat pattern. It's just a matter of time before he shoves her away again, because *a boy becomes a male over his mother's dead body*.[1]

It's almost as if the thirteen-year-old must "kill" his mother until he's sure he has been released from her grasp. Of course, he doesn't do this all at once. He persistently makes stabs at Mom all year, and never wipes up the blood. He doesn't realize why he acts this way toward his mother; he simply feels driven to protect his separate identity.

At times the thirteen-year-old boy indulges in private worries and makes detailed criticisms of his parents. Children this age are "on the lookout for evidences of hypocrisy in their parents. To the extent that their parents are obviously sincere in their ideals, their children feel under obligation to continue to adhere to them. But if they can find hypocrisy, this relieves them of the moral duty to conform. It also gives them a welcome opportunity to reproach their parents."[2]

This rivalry between a son and his mother is similar to the rivalry that developed when he was between four and six. It's more intense now because the thirteen-year-old has stronger emotions and senses he is almost an adult. Soon he will compete in his parents' league, so he periodically feels he must elbow his parents off their seat of power. One school of psychology says that "boys who feel overawed by their fathers suppress their resentment and antagonism toward him and displace it onto their mothers . . . flaring up at her over quite reasonable requests or imagined slights."[3]

It's not uncommon for a thirteen-year-old boy to think, "I worry that people won't like me. . . . I worry that I'm going to worry. I worry that I should stop worrying."[4] Actually these worries are a sign of inward awareness, which is a major sign of maturity at this stage of adolescence.

Healthy Peer-Group Pressure

Most mothers are aware of the demands peer-group pressure places on their sons. While they push away from Mom and Dad, they need intimate ties with friends of the same age. These ties begin with those of the same sex and eventually switch to those of the opposite sex. These friendships give them support while they are giving up the identity of being their parents' child and forming their own identity. A mother's reassurances may fall on deaf ears if his peers don't like or won't accept him in their groups.

I've noticed that thirteen-year-old boys are embarrassed to be seen with their mothers in public. They will ask to be let out of the car before they actually reach their destination, unless Mom is driving a showy car they want their friends to see.

Most mothers worry about the mesmerizing power peer groups seem to hold over their sons, because the group's influence is out of their control. But actually, the peer group has a very positive function in a boy's adjustment to adulthood. At a time when he is plagued with many worries, he can gain great comfort and consolation knowing other boys his age are struggling with similar challenges.

I overheard a conversation recently where one boy was amazed and delighted to discover that his friend had some of the same feelings he did. He told his buddy, "My mom always gets on my case about my room and says I don't take good care of my things." His friend replied, "Really! My mom used to do that to me, too. I just told her it wasn't my fault I was born. Now she leaves me alone." Even though I didn't like the response that was given, I could tell that each boy lost some of his feelings of aloneness and peculiarity and gained a pleasurable sense of belonging through this chat. Boys can emerge out of adolescence as much stronger young adults when they spend time with their peers and family rather than just with their family.

Good peer-group pressure will work for the child if he is involved in a group that esteems good ideals and morals. This is where parents can use their God-given responsibility as overseers to protect their children from poor influences and help them form healthy friendships. I've talked with many parents who have made drastic changes for the sake of their young teenagers. Some have moved their children from public to private schools. Others have decided to attend a church where youth group activities are a priority. I remember a well-known psychologist saying, with a twinkle in his eye, "I hate to leave my own denomination, but I'm looking for the church with the largest gymnasium I can find. I'm raising boys." His decision paid off; his boys identified with the peer group at the new church and enthusiastically attended the youth activities.

Boys and Their Dads

I recently talked with a thirteen-year-old friend I hadn't seen for a while.

"How are you doing these days?" I asked.

"I'm okay."

"How's your family?"

"They're fine, but my dad is overseas again."

"You seem sad. I know you must miss him."

"I miss Dad a lot. I wish he didn't have to be gone so much. Mom says he just chooses to take these overseas assignments. But school is great. I've made more friends this year than last year, and I've got some neat teachers, too."

Randy had plunged into two of the most important areas of his life: his relationships with his dad and his friends. This is typical for most thirteen-year-old boys.

Boys this age desperately need love and affirmation from their fathers. I know a thirteen-year-old boy who learned everything about the bus system in his state, completely by himself, so he could visit his father who lives in another location. He craved his father's acceptance and care.

Years ago I worked with a boy who was very depressed, unable to concentrate in school, and flunking his classes. Among other problems, Cedric had terribly low self-esteem. After talking with his mother, I began to understand why. Cedric's father was infuriated over Cedric's lack of interest in sports. In his father's eyes, Cedric was a complete failure. His poor school performance made matters worse. I met with Cedric's father to discuss his son's problems.

After I greeted Mr. Jaben, he said, "You're wasting your time trying to counsel that boy. He's no good."

"Your son is very despondent and must have help," I replied.

"Well, don't expect me to do anything," he retorted.

"Mr. Jaben, you may be the only person who can help Cedric. He desperately needs your approval and feels you hate him."

"Frankly, ma'am, I think I do. The boy is no good, causes endless arguments in our marriage, and has nearly broken up our home."

"How can a little thirteen-year-old boy do that to you?"
I inquired.

"My wife blames me for his problems and accuses me of
being cruel."

"Mr. Jaben, I believe Cedric must have a better relationship with you before he will make any progress at all. His
problems are serious."

Completely irritated, he barked back at me, "When I
don't perform well at work, my boss doesn't cater to my
feelings. He says, 'Make some improvements or don't
bother coming back.' That kid had better shape up and
face the real world, whether he feels like it or not!"

"Would it be possible for you to give him some encouragement along the way and the security of knowing you
care about him?"

"He has to earn my respect first. What sort of father
would I be if I never expected anything out of him? If he
shapes up, then maybe some encouragement is in order."

I didn't feel Mr. Jaben understood the urgency of his
son's needs when we talked that afternoon. It was a very
difficult case for me as a counselor, because there was so
little I could do to help Cedric. The only thing that
seemed to matter to him was his father's loving approval.
During one of our meetings, I said to this deprived little
boy, "Cedric, I absolutely agree with you. Your dad does
not show any interest in you, and this is awful. But your
mother loves you very much. She would do anything to
give you the extra love that your father will not give
you."

I'll never forget the answer he gave me: "If a boy's
mother loves him, it's no big deal. A mother would love
you even if you were a murderer. So that doesn't count. If
your father thinks you're okay, then you're a great person.
My dad says I'm no good, so what's the use of anything?"

As a member of a family, a child internalizes the ideas
and attitudes expressed by the significant people in his
life. He comes to see himself in the same way his loved

ones see him. In this sense, his family acts as a mirror. The only adult male in Cedric's life told him he was no good, and Cedric believed it. Cedric internalized the labels his father gave him and grew up convinced he was worthless. Unfortunately this particular family was not involved with a church or community organization where other fathers could have given Cedric the love and attention he needed.

When Dad Lives Somewhere Else

Over the years I have worked with many divorced families and seen a common occurrence among thirteen-year-old boys. Many youngsters this age beg to live with their father rather than their mother. I wish there were something I could say to mothers to ease the pain these requests inflict. I don't have a magic wand, but I do know these desires don't surface because Mom is a poor parent. Neither is it a sign that the boy doesn't love his mother. These requests usually come because an adolescent thinks his dad is richer and will give him nice things. Some boys have a deep fear of becoming an adult male and think they will feel more secure with their fathers. If a boy dislikes or feels uncomfortable with a new stepfather, he may also reason that life would be better at his real dad's house.

I've seen this happen time after time and usually suggest the boy try living with his father for a season, as long as the arrangement doesn't disrupt his school progress. Over 90 percent of these boys will beg their moms to take them back long before the prolonged visit is completed. They realize they need their mothers' love more than any physical advantage offered by the other household. If a boy is given the chance to miss his mother, he is likely to settle the issue for himself. He finds he is the one making the choice to live with his mother, and now he has the advantage of knowing what he really wants. Many times the issue is never raised again and the boy is content with periodic visits to his father's home.

The Thirteen-Year-Old and Trust

Several years ago I was asked to talk with a junior-high group at a large church in our area. The youth leaders were concerned about some of the teenagers' activities and attitudes toward their parents. I opened our session with a discussion time. The youngsters were very cooperative and talked freely with me about their activities and relationships with Mom and Dad. I must admit I was surprised by some of the things I heard. I was expecting something different from this conservative churchgoing bunch of kids.

I started out by asking, "How many of you consider yourselves to be honest with your parents?"

No one raised a hand. There was total silence as the teens looked around at others in the group.

"I'm not sure I understand your silence. Are you all telling me that you're dishonest?"

"We don't see it that way. We don't actually lie. We just don't tell them all the facts."

"Why?" I replied.

One guy stood up and said, "If we told them everything, we would never get to do anything. Besides, it takes too long to explain things to them. If we tell them just the basics, then they don't worry as much or keep asking questions. What they don't know won't hurt them."

It sounded to me that they were making unreasonable requests of their parents and they needed to prove they could be trusted. I'm not sure I convinced them of anything that night, but we spent the rest of our time discussing how they could earn their parents' trust. I encourage parents of junior-high children to talk with them about earning trust, too. Some of the things that can be brought into this kind of discussion are listed below.

Teens need to be instructed to:

- Develop a habit of telling the truth, no matter how painful it may be at the time. This will protect them from building a reputation as a liar.
- Try very hard to show an attitude of cooperation with those in authority. If they work at being willing to "get along," they'll be less likely to argue or rebel just for the heck of it.
- Keep their word in any agreement. If they tell someone they will be somewhere at a certain time, they should be there.
- Be somewhere when they say they will be there. (Many teens admit that they ask permission to go to the house of a friend their mother likes. From there, they go off with kids they know their mom doesn't trust.)
- Call home and report any change of plans to their parents. Sometimes they may need to ask permission to do something, but even if they don't, it's a sign of courtesy to keep in touch with the home front.
- Respect the special rules of their particular home, even if their peers don't have the same rules.
- Be responsible for taking care of their possessions. If they lose a jacket, for example, they should do the best they can to find it on their own.
- Show some effort at school. If their parents see them trying to get decent grades, they will be more likely to trust them in other areas.

Many teens will respond to this kind of discussion with, "What do you think I am, some perfect kid who does everything right?" They need to be assured that even when they make small steps toward these ideals, they will be proving they can be trusted. Trying is the first step to achievement.

Thirteen's Not Forever

Most mothers usher in the fourteenth year of their sons' lives with a hip-hip hurrah! Overnight, their irritable thirteen-year-old seems to become a different person. He's healthy, energetic, and expressive, and his whole approach to life is more friendly, outgoing, contented, and relaxed.

At thirteen, he was withdrawn. He ruminated and worked hard to understand his changing moods. "The inwardizing, self-absorption of thirteen served to enrich the structure of the self which now becomes more fully integrated and in better balance with other personalities. Fourteen is therefore better oriented both to himself and to his interpersonal environment."[5] It seems he has moved beyond the touchiness and constant criticism of his mom and family that was apparent at thirteen. Down moods disappear faster and, being full of fun, he is an enjoyable person to have around the house.

But life still has its challenges. Fourteen-year-old boys worry about their bodies. If they're small, it's threatening to see their friends grow quickly while they remain the same size. They are also preoccupied with their sexual development. Most boys have experienced ejaculation, probably through masturbating, by the time they are fourteen. They're ready to discuss these issues, and it's very important they be properly informed, whether they ask questions or not.

Travis transitioned smoothly into his fourteenth year. From a rather grumpy thirteen-year-old, he changed into a congenial young man and began making many friends at school and church. His mother, Jane, said, "I actually have to make appointments with my son in order to see him. His schedule is constantly full of activities with his friends!" Like most mothers of fourteen-year-olds, Jane is concerned about the amount of time Travis spends away from home. It's hard for her to know where he is, who he's with, and what he's doing twenty-four hours a day. The long summer was especially difficult for her because she works full-time and Travis detests the idea of a baby-sitter. She worked out a system where he reported to a neighbor "supervisor" throughout the day while she was at the office.

Travis fits the profile of a fourteen-year-old in many areas. He is much more rational and logical than he was at thirteen. He uses his mind to reason and is rapidly developing a broad vocabulary. With this new command of language skills, he has become interested in the solar system, outer space investigation, mechanical gadgets, and a host of other areas where his parents have no knowledge.

Whenever my husband cannot figure out how to fix something on our car, his first solution is to call our fourteen-year-old grandson, Jack, who seems to have instinctive knowledge of cars and mechanics. We had to chuckle last week when he said, "Poppa, just look under the dashboard and find a little lever that can be turned on or off." Then, in a patronizing voice, he spouted, "I better explain all this to you when I see you. It's really not hard to understand."

Jack, like many other boys his age, quickly assimilates knowledge. Whenever I am around boys this age, I want to ask, "What's new? Tell me what you are learning this week." They are usually full of facts, and their minds are expanding with each passing day. However, their high level of sociability doesn't always enhance their school performance. With their attention pulled in so many new directions, it's easy for them to goof off, talk, and not complete assignments.

Although most boys are happier and more positive at fourteen, there are still the everlasting problems of coming in on time at night, completing homework, taking care of clothing and rooms, and helping around the house. Younger siblings don't seem to be as irritating as in earlier years, but a fourteen-year-old still hates it when anyone tampers with his possessions.

Outside the family, they have great fun with friends. They love social gatherings and mix well with both boys and girls. Girls this age tend to want to date one special boy, but boys aren't as interested yet. They like girls but don't want to be tied down to one person for any length of time. Roughhousing and hard competitive play between boys and girls is common.

Many fourteen-year-old boys claim to believe in God and have some concept of who He is. They generally enjoy church if they are raised in a churchgoing family, and are somewhat interested in youth-group activities. Youth leaders I have interviewed seem to agree that it is usually older age groups who show a deeper interest in spiritual truths, but this doesn't mean a younger teen's spiritual development shouldn't be cultivated.

A teenager's sexual attitudes and behavior can be greatly affected by his religious beliefs. A fourteen-year-old may feel very strongly that sexual intercourse is wrong outside of marriage, because of his religious convictions.

However, a boy's spiritual beliefs don't generally seem to affect his overall behavior at this age. One fourteen-year-old boy loved his church youth group and attended every activity offered. But one evening when he returned home after Bible study, he stole $40.00 from his mother. His justification for his behavior was, "She owed it to me for all the work I've done around the house."

Thinking It Through

1. Some mothers say they experience great frustrations when their sons are thirteen. Why?

2. Do you believe there is an instinctive drive within the thirteen-year-old to emancipate himself from his mother?

3. Discuss the statement that a boy becomes a male over his mother's dead body.

4. What are some creative ways parents can use healthy peer-group pressure to help shape their sons?

5. Many thirteen-year-olds from broken homes beg to live with their "other" parent. When might this be a good idea and when might it be bad?

6. What are some things you have done with your children to help them earn your trust?

7. Do you agree that most boys at fourteen have spiritual beliefs, but these beliefs don't generally seem to affect their overall behavior?

8. What did you learn from this chapter that you can share with another mother? Whom will you encourage? When?

5

Little Boys Are
Sexually Aware ▪▪

I'm amazed at the scores of mothers I've met who have
limited or no understanding of the normal sexual development of little boys. They're ashamed when their sons
handle their genitals. They're baffled by their little boys'
erections, masturbation, and wet dreams.

In this chapter I want to present facts without interpre-
tation or moralizing. Mothers need to know what to
expect. When you are planning a journey through life
with a son, it helps to have a road map with signs that tell
you what's ahead. This chapter will discuss the phases of
a boy's sexual journey from birth to sixteen years of age.

For many years some authorities had an erroneous idea
of how children develop sexually. They thought that
during the first seven years, children were oblivious to
sexual feelings. During the next seven years, sexual awareness supposedly went "underground" (and adults were to
make sure it did). This was called the latency period. After
latency, boys were somehow "awakened" and became
sexually active as adolescents.

Today we know this is not the case. Both male and
female babies as young as four to six months have

orgasms. Male infants have been observed lying on their stomachs and pushing themselves so their penis is stimulated. As soon as a baby boy can coordinate his movements, he plays with his penis, and he learns very early that it is a pleasurable sensation.[1]

Many mothers are concerned when their sons explore themselves. "I have a nasty little monster on my hands!" they exclaim. But this is a very normal part of male development. The child is becoming aware of all the parts of his body, including his sex organs. If a mother is particularly anxious about these activities, a game or toy will quickly distract young children from stimulating themselves.

Why Does My Little Boy Have So Many Erections?

It's important for mothers to understand that when a small boy has an erection, it's not necessarily a sexual response. There are many nonsexual stimulating sources, such as:[2]

excitement	water of a shower
sudden fright	lying on a beach
friction of clothes over penis	diving or swimming
	anxiety about a test
pressure of pants while sitting	seeing a policeman
	watching a fire
punishment	playing an exciting game
riding a bike	urination
any fast motion	straining the bowels
vibration from a vehicle	lifting heavy loads

Erections can also happen when a boy is sexually stimulated in a direct manner, such as:

seeing a particular girl	sexy jokes
watching girls	erotic pictures
thinking about girls	climbing a tree

sex play with children	reading books
dancing	watching others being affec-
looking at their bodies	tionate
looking at other boys' or-	rubbing with a towel
gans	sliding down banisters
daydreaming	

Erections are only one small piece of the male sexuality puzzle. Below I have highlighted various other characteristics of a boy's sexual development from birth to age sixteen, in part based on the findings of Gesell, Ilg, and Ames, in their books *Infant and Child in the Culture of Today, The Child From Five to Ten,* and *Youth: The Years from Ten to Sixteen.*

Birth to one year

• Genital erections can happen when a baby is still in his mother's womb.
• At ten months, a baby boy grasps his genitals.
• A small percentage of babies have orgasms after four months.
• A small percentage of baby boys will thrust or rock themselves to stimulate their penis because they have learned the pleasurable sensations attached to these moves.

At two and a half

• A boy this age is very aware of his sex organs and handles them.
• They are aware of the differences between females and males. They will look at undressed females, but usually won't talk about it.

At three

• A three-year-old boy will talk about male and female differences.
• Boys this age have the desire to look at and touch adults. They are genuinely interested in their mothers' breasts, and will often reach for or stare at them.

- They begin to show interest in knowing the origin of babies.

At four

- A four-year-old boy tends to grab his penis when under stress or when he wants to urinate.
- Some boys this age get involved in sex play, mostly by showing their genitals to others or by playing doctor.
- There is a preoccupation with bathroom activities, and boys will urinate in the presence of others at this age.
- Though they will ask where babies come from, they are not very interested in knowing all the facts.

At five

- Boys tend to be more modest in this stage. They don't expose themselves to others as much.
- There is a keen awareness of adult sex differences.
- They continue to ask about the origin of babies.

At six

- The child becomes more aware of male and female differences.
- Sex play such as exhibitionism in play or in the bathroom at school is common.
- Some little boys this age become upset about the idea of procreation.
- They ask many questions about their sexual organs.

At seven

- Sex play continues and tends to increase at this age.
- The child is very interested in babies, their origin, and their birth.
- The little boy may have a sweetheart or girlfriend.
- If a child lives in a rural area, he will be fascinated with watching animals mate.

At eight

- Boys and girls respond to each others' attractions at this age.
- The young boy becomes very interested in sex. He explores the topic, asks questions, and is interested in peeping.
- There is curiosity about smutty jokes and sex words.
- When they watch animals and birds mate, they dissociate these actions from what humans do to procreate.

At nine

- The young boy becomes much more private about his body, especially with his mother.
- The child may try to kiss a girl, but usually he is very embarrassed and tries to avoid girls. Signs like "No Girls Allowed!" posted on his bedroom door are typical.
- Talk about sex becomes more explicit, and perhaps vulgar. This is the age when a neighbor may complain about a little boy's language.

At ten

- Sex play continues. Dirty jokes are told, but the child often doesn't know the real meaning of what he is saying.
- This is sexually a very quiet year for many boys.

At eleven

- Erections occur frequently.
- Advanced boys show puberty changes.
- One-fourth of all boys will grow taller at a faster rate this year.
- This is a "fat" period, when boys will tend to look chubby around their hips and chest.
- Heavy bone growth occurs now.
- Genitals become larger for fast-growing boys.
- Pubic hair begins to grow.
- A boy can be stimulated now by watching animals mate.

- About 50 percent or more of all boys will masturbate at this age.

At twelve

- There is an increased growth in sex organs.
- Boys are more interested in sex.
- Erections often occur spontaneously as a result of stimulation.
- Some boys keep pictures of nudes around.
- Masturbation is practiced alone or in groups.
- Less mature twelve-year-olds indulge in sex play.
- A boy this age usually doesn't like instructions about sex from his parents. He will listen better to an objective counselor.
- Boys seek out sex information in many ways.
- Sex is discussed with other boys.
- Sex jokes are exchanged with other children.
- Boys enjoy being with girls and want to go to parties with them.

At thirteen

- A rapid growth of genitals occurs.
- A boy's voice deepens and sometimes cracks.
- There is a growth spurt in height, and boys become concerned with their growth in height.
- Erections continue to occur spontaneously and with direct stimulation.
- Boys tend to be very direct and clumsy in their social contact with girls.
- Many boys like to wear athletic supports.

At fourteen

- A boy's size continues to increase rapidly.
- His body becomes more muscle and less fat.
- The deepening of his voice may happen slowly or suddenly.

- A large majority of boys will have an ejaculation by the end of the fourteenth year, generally due to masturbation.
- Nocturnal emissions (wet dreams) occur and cause embarrassment to the boy.
- Boys need and like sexual instruction and discussion at this age.
- They must be taught self-control concerning their sexual involvements with girls.

At fifteen

- Ninety-five percent of their adult height has been reached.
- Their genitals are nearly adult size.
- Dancing is very stimulating.
- Masturbation increases for some.
- Sexual daydreaming is common.

At sixteen

- Some boys stop growth here, others may add up to six inches.
- Strong sexual impulses are difficult for them to control.
- Masturbation may be frequent.
- Erotic stimulation from looking at pictures and reading sex novels is common.
- Daydreams tend to be erotic and stimulating.
- Physical contact with girls markedly increases.

What About Masturbation?

Authorities agree that most boys masturbate. The Gesell Institute, which is famous for its research on children, reports that various forms of masturbating movements occur in little boys before the age of five. Tiny children find it pleasurable to stimulate themselves. Mothers report that masturbation occurs more frequently when a child seems to feel neglected, lonely, or unloved. Perhaps the stimulation serves as a substitute for the attention he wants. But even if the child is not deprived of attention, he may masturbate simply because he likes the sensation. A well-known psychiatry manual says: "There exists a general seeking for pleasurable activity of a sexual type. Masturbation as an auto erotic activity is universal in youngsters and originates in their simple discovery that manipulation of their genitals is pleasurable."[3]

Some children masturbate after they are put to bed at night, especially if they have not had enough physical exercise to drain their energies during the day. Since playing with toys and other diversions usually aren't permitted after bedtime, some amuse themselves through stimulating their sex organs.

During the last decade, much attention has been focused on the problem of sexual abuse within families, where older siblings or relatives engage in sex play with younger ones. Inappropriate exposure to sex may result in increased masturbation in boys and men.[4]

Authorities suggest that some young boys may masturbate to "get back" at an overreactive parent who uses cruel punishment. The child thinks, "If they knew what I was doing, they would be furious. . . . I'll do it anyway!" The child uses masturbation to release tension and anger after a fallout with his parents.

In most cases, masturbation is a passing phase for children. Their physical health is not adversely affected, except that fear of detection or criticism may interfere with sleep and appetite. Masturbation is harmful mainly to the child's moral and emotional well-being. When practiced to excess, it can lead to self-reproach, a loss of self-esteem, and feelings of guilt. Fear of discovery may result in undesirable secrecy.[5]

There are several things a mother can do to keep masturbation in check. She can structure the child's world so that opportunities for masturbation are limited. Small children can be taught to sleep with their hands outside the covers. Little boys can wear trousers without

pockets and be discouraged from playi͏
isolated places.

Outlets for the child's energy should be ͏
his time fully occupied. A regular daily
plenty of exercise and wholesome social co͏
aid in overcoming the habit. Cooperative and competitive
play is important, so the child is physically tired when he
goes to bed and will fall asleep quickly. Children who
have numerous contacts with good moral friends have
little need to resort to masturbation. Little boys should
also get up promptly upon awaking in the morning, since
erotic fancies are frequently indulged in at this time.

Some pediatricians suggest small children be told,
"Masturbation is for babies (like thumb sucking) and you
are too grown up to continue this." If a teenager
masturbates, it does not help to scold him or frighten him
with tales of terrible consequences such as insanity or
disease. Imposed shame, guilt, and loss of self-respect
will only make the habit more difficult to overcome and
encourage secrecy.

A successful approach to the treatment of masturbation
is through a moral and intellectual understanding of the
adolescent. The teenager must be assured that the act is
not physically harmful but does have some negative
aspects. It may help to explain these disadvantages, such
as time and energy loss, the resultant worry and shame,
the fears about others finding out, and unhealthy fanta-
sizing. He should be assured that he can stop masturbating if he will try and that there are other more rewarding
outlets for his energies. Parents must keep in mind that
the habit may be an expression of deeper unhappiness,
and reasons should be sought as to why the child may feel
disturbed.

Children need to know not only the physiological facts
about sex, but also the moral obligations that make sexual
control necessary. A boy has natural curiosity about
himself and a certain amount of sex enlightenment from

.om or Dad may help him manage a situation better than if he is left ignorant.

Shield Boys From Inappropriate Sexual Stimuli

It's important that little boys be encouraged to develop in certain ways and also guarded from certain sources of stimulation. This should be a quiet phase where children are not exposed to sexually provocative material.

When I was a child, the women in my community who wanted to get married and bear children had the luxury of being full-time homemakers. There were few cultural influences or opportunities that pulled women out of the home. Children not only had their mothers around most of the time, but also had additional supervision from hired help.

As a small child, I was sexually ignorant and never enlightened by adults. If I asked my parents about sex, I was told, "Hush, hush! You must not talk about these things. You don't need to know about such matters at your age. Only bad little girls ask those questions."

When I was nine years old, a friend told me that her mother kept "scandal" magazines from England in their outdoor shed. "They are full of pictures and stories for grown-ups. Whenever Mom isn't around, I sneak out to the shed and read them," she confided. Since we didn't have the same classes at school, we only saw each other once a week at church. I begged her for that dubious grown-up material, and the next Sunday she tore out some pages from the older magazines, stuffed them in her bloomers, and slipped them to me at church. I crammed them in my Bible and ran home, hid in my room, and looked at the revealing pictures! Eventually my source dried up because one of the younger children in her family tattled.

I was terribly upset with my mother a few months later when she refused to let me go to my friend's house for a birthday party. She never told me why I couldn't go except, "We don't know them very well, and I have never visited in their home." Now I am very thankful my mother was careful about supervising my friendships when I was small.

When I was about eleven, I vacationed with a relative on a big farm for health reasons. The climate was good, and my parents thought this would be best for my well-being. One afternoon I found a large pile of magazines with passionate love stories in an old storage barn. I used to sneak away for hours and read the romantic tales, until I got caught in the act. Even after I was scolded and told to stay away from that material, I still found ways to read them. Those stories had a remarkable hold on me. You've heard the saying, "Out of sight, out of mind." That wasn't true with these magazines. It was almost like an addiction. All I wanted to do was withdraw into the fantasy world of these flowery narratives. My point is, it's best not to have romance books and sexually provocative reading material within a child's reach. As a kid, I also remember hearing lurid stories from the hired help that worked around our home. This kind of talk made me fearful of becoming an adult. I think there's a parallel here: Mothers must guard their sons from overexposure to older children who make them uneasy. When they sense something isn't right, it's important they listen to their inner voices and not say to themselves, "I must be crazy, fretting about Johnny being with so and so. I shouldn't be such a suspicious worrier!"

Mothers must listen to their intuition about baby-sitters, too. If younger children must be left with someone, it's important that the character of the caretaker and the surroundings be thoroughly investigated. What children will your son be exposed to while he is under the baby-sitter's supervision? You don't want sexually precocious older children stimulating your young, vulnerable little boy with dirty talk and jokes.

I strongly advocate that mothers check out the homes their children want to visit, even if it causes them some embarrassment. It's best that a mother endure a little interpersonal discomfort so her son's sexual development isn't tainted with perversion. I recall one young boy from a splendid Christian home who regularly visited a neighbor's home. He loved spending time with the older boys in that household, but they began exposing him to highly explicit sexual material. This continued for a long period of time and may have seriously damaged this little boy's emotional and spiritual development. It saddens me that these mothers never knew what their sons were doing.

I have asked scores of young parents what they do to control the sexual stimulation of their young children. Many have mentioned taking drastic measures to monitor the influence of TV and radio. A few have sold their televisions. Others forbid TV viewing after a certain time in the evening because sensual shows are broadcast during later hours.

I am in hearty agreement with their controls. TV can turn into an enemy of family communication if it isn't monitored. A child's proper development can be hindered by media crammed with violence, sexual acts, and innuendos. Did you know that by the age of fourteen, the average boy has watched about 18,000 murders on TV?[6]

It's also important for mothers to choose their words carefully when discussing their son's playmates. I cringe when I hear a mother boast to her friends about her cute little son and his girlfriends. Without realizing it, she may be encouraging and arousing sexual interests before the proper time.

I know it's impossible for a mother to monitor what her son sees and hears around the clock. But she mustn't focus on what she can't do. Rather she must consider what she can do and set limits to protect him from harmful overexposure.

Modesty at Home Is a Must

When boys are six and older, it's vitally important that mothers be modest. It's unhealthy for mothers to be excessively intimate with their sons at this age. If a mother is nude in front of her son, it suggests she does not recognize his maleness.

Perhaps you disagree with me and say, "What's wrong with exposing bodies in a close family unit? The human body is beautiful, and all this cover-up seems unnecessary. It's good for boys to be accustomed to a naked female body in a protected environment."

I must be direct on this issue because I have seen the results of immodesty. During the years I've followed the lives of small boys into adulthood, I've noticed homosexual tendencies occasionally have developed in boys who had mothers who were not careful in this area. The mothers undressed in front of their sons and used the bathroom in their presence, even when the boys were well into adolescence.

Dr. Harvey Kaufman, a well-known child psychiatrist, taught me that mothers should get out of the bathroom when their seven-year-old boys are undressing and taking a bath. Modesty is more important than a thoroughly scrubbed back. Natural instincts need to be governed and directed so the child isn't absorbed and controlled by them. A little boy who is constantly bombarded with sexually stimulating material may show little interest in intellectual learning because too much of his energy and concentration is moving in another direction.

But what if my son wanders into my bedroom while I am putting on my bra? What should I do? I suggest a low-key approach. Say something simple, like, "Hey, can't you knock at my door? I'm in the middle of getting dressed." He'll get the message.

Mother-Son Affection

Bob was a very bright nine-year-old boy who was flunking school. He constantly clowned around and disrupted other boys during class with obscene language and pictures. After seeing a therapist for a number of weeks, Bob told his counselor that he liked the times when his mother held him. Bob said, "I wait until my stepfather leaves the house and then Mom and I cuddle up on the couch together and watch TV."[7] Eventually the therapist discovered that the mother did more than watch TV with her son. In a seductive sort of way, she caressed him and gave him body massages. The therapist diagnosed Bob as possibly being prehomosexual.

I realize children desperately need affection. In fact, most disturbed boys have been deprived of appropriate affection. I've met boys who were never hugged or told "I love you" during their childhood. I am not advocating that parents don't hug.

I am suggesting, however, that mothers be careful how they express affection to their sons during latency. Some little boys try to fondle their mothers' bodies in very intimate ways. Mothers have reported their sons constantly wanting to stare at or touch their breasts. These are times when a mother can simply say to her son, "I don't like you touching me there. We can give bear hugs to each other or a kiss on the cheek, but don't touch me there." It might be helpful for her to demonstrate a bear hug to her son. She must set the structure for the right kind of affection.

It is inappropriate for a parent or child to become physically aroused while caressing each other. Nowadays, back rubbing seems to be a popular activity in many households. I'm not sure this is wise between parents and children of the opposite sex. It's fine between husbands and wives, but I suggest caution must be taken when massaging becomes a free-for-all among family members.

When and How Should I Talk to My Son?

Sometimes it's hard for parents to talk with their children about sex. How should the conversation be started? What are the right and wrong things to say? Dr. Kirk Douglass, M.D., a leading Christian pediatrician on the West Coast, offers some excellent suggestions:

We are all sexual beings, and sex education begins at day one. If you follow a two- to four-year-old around the house, you'll see his day is a clutter of toys, books, cookies, and stairs. The time he spends on any task is very short, therefore anything related to his sexuality is more reflective than verbal.

When the child reaches the age of four to six, he develops better verbal and motor skills. Language development will contain some new words that can cause negative reactions in parents. These are usually the same words the parents cooed to their little darling when he was a tiny tot, but now they become a tool in the child's hand during power struggles. And, my, how they can use them! As with most things, this too shall pass, if given the proper focus and time. It's normal for them to want to explore their own body parts as well as those of others at this age.

Parents should explain to their kids that people are made differently, particularly males and females, and this is God's design. The private parts of our bodies are just that—private, and only for family to see. Detailed explanations are outside the understanding of most children this age.

Talking with the seven- to ten-year-old requires a different approach. This age group develops a high degree of modesty that is appropriate. Girls don't like to take off their T-shirts, and boys want Mom to leave the room when they get undressed. The seven- to ten-year-old asks direct questions and wants direct answers. "What is an erection?" "How do babies get inside Mommy?" Simple but direct answers are best.

Boys and girls are developing on different time lines. Puberty begins earlier for girls than boys, and by the age of ten, early breast budding occurs. Boys are still trying to stay up on skateboards. A discussion with little girls about secondary sexual development is in order now. She must learn that menstruation will not occur for almost two years after puberty begins. It's frightening for a fourth grader to suddenly notice her breasts developing if she is unaware that this doesn't mean she'll be grown-up overnight. The prospect of maturity, with all its problems, can be anxiety producing for children.

Along with the anatomical changes come the emotional and hormonal changes. It now behooves parents to carefully instruct their daughter about modesty of dress and to make sure they know where she is at all times. Children this age ask few questions about sex. A good way to open a conversation with them is, "I'll bet you have had some questions about the changes in your body lately." Most boys this age couldn't care less about talking with Mom and Dad about sex. They are more concerned about a new pair of skis or a new skateboard.

The eleven- to fourteen-year-old girl is becoming an adult physically, but psychologically is only a teenager. By this age, most children have garnered facts about sex from friends and family. They have almost all of the information, but little of the whys. The morality they have learned at home is put to the test in adolescence.

Boys and girls must be treated differently at this age. Boys are worried about their developing breast tissue. Many parents bring their eleven- to fourteen-year-old sons in to me for reassurance that the male breast tissue enlargement of this age is normal. Girls should be told that their menstrual periods for the first year or two are likely to be irregular. It's okay to use tampons if they are active, but they should be taught the dangers of leaving them in for extended periods of time.

Thinking It Through

1. What are your thoughts about masturbation?

2. How have you dealt with the topic of sex with your children?

3. Do you think mothers should discuss sex with adolescent boys? Explain.

4. What do you think about the idea, "Modesty for mothers is a must"? Explain.

5. Do you feel impressed to change anything about your approach to mothering? What is one step you can take to implement that change?

6. If you were to pass on some information you learned from this chapter, who would you talk with, and what would you say?

6

Homosexuality: It Happens in Christian Families, Too

———————————————————— ▪▪

"I'm still shocked," Marie anxiously exclaimed as she set her teacup on the table. "I never dreamed anything like this would take place in our family," she continued. "Jeff was such a good little boy. How could this happen?" Jeff had announced during Christmas vacation that he was a homosexual. "My husband calls him a traitor and won't have anything to do with him. I don't know how I feel. *Numb* is a good word. I just can't believe it.

"Where did I go wrong? Why didn't I see he needed help? He grew up in a loving Christian home and had good friends. He was the most spiritually sensitive of our children, too. We all thought he had a great future ahead of him. I don't know what will happen now. Life will never be the same."

I tried to help this mother understand that no one has any pat answers. There wasn't an easy explanation for her son's choice. She and her husband were happily married and very involved in their four children's lives. Nevertheless, Jeff had chosen a sexual preference different from the rest of his family's.

Boys who become homosexuals come from all kinds of families, and Christian households are not exempt. That's why we must look the issue squarely in the face. Homosexuality has appeared in great and noble families throughout history. It's a universal problem, and Christian mothers must not hide their heads and say, "It will never happen to one of my kids!" It does happen in strong families, and sometimes there appears to be no discernible reason why a son chooses a sexual preference outside the norm. Sometimes the tendencies are seen at such an early age that it appears to have been inborn.[1]

In this chapter I want to review leading theories about the development of homosexual behavior. This is a complicated subject, and all the answers are not in yet. Professionals agree that there is no single cause of homosexuality; it is a multifaceted problem. Experts offer their own, sometimes conflicting, theories for homosexual orientation.

Sociologists generally attribute homosexual preference to social influences outside the family circle and various learning experiences. When the nature versus nurture question is raised, they point to the effect of environment on an individual. Homosexuality is explained as a learned phenomenon without any physiological base. They propose that people are born with no particular predisposition and sexuality is channeled by various learning experiences. Some sociologists claim a high rate of success in converting homosexuals to being heterosexual.

Psychoanalysts view homosexuality as a psychological disorder. The father of psychoanalysis, Sigmund Freud, believed homosexuality was virtually untreatable.

Geneticists and psychophysiologists look to biological factors for an explanation. Some theorize that boys are programmed at birth to become either homosexual or heterosexual, regardless of social circumstances. They propose that certain youngsters, beginning in early childhood, have a remarkably clear homosexual orientation. Such a child's entire approach to life is homosexual.

Those adhering to the hormonal theory say that homosexual development is linked to levels of hormones. Homosexuals have lower levels of male hormones than heterosexuals, and their ratio of male hormones is also different.

Alfred Kinsey, a professor at the University of Indiana, studied 5300 men and communicated his results in a report entitled "Sexual Behavior in the Human Male." This was the first large empirical study on male sexuality of its kind. Kinsey's findings are not inconsistent with the biological theory for sexual preference. His studies suggest that exclusive homosexuals did not seem to learn the role. Rather it seemed to come from an early predisposition that emerged during childhood. Their lack of conformity may have caused family reactions. For instance, if a boy did not act masculine, he may have turned from his father who insisted that he be "macho." The father may have then withdrawn emotionally from his son and become hostile. The son in turn became bitter and would not identify with his father. Kinsey suggests an inborn predisposition toward gender nonconformity *may lead to* rather than *proceed from* the kinds of family relationships that have been traditionally held responsible for gender nonconformity.[2]

Other experts reject this theory and say that research overwhelmingly indicates homosexuals are not born, they are bred. Albert Ellis, a psychologist who is not friendly to Christianity, examines several theories that describe the cause of homosexuality in his book *Homosexuality: Its Cause and Its Cure.* Included are the *theories* that homosexuality is genetically caused, that it is hormonally based, that it is directly connected with the person's body build, that it is the result of brain damage, that it is culturally and historically uniform in incidence, and that it is completely untreatable. Dr. Ellis concluded, "When critically reviewed, all these hypotheses are seen to be unsupported by objective, confirmatory evidence of a scientific nature."[3]

Psychologists say homosexuality is primarily a learned or acquired response pattern in a child who comes from a dysfunctional family. There may also be predisposing genetic or biological factors in some cases that make a child more vulnerable to learning homosexual behavior. Many homosexuals have had an unhealthy relationship with their opposite sex parent. As a result, they have major issues of unresolved anger with persons of the opposite gender.

Although the theories above vary, proponents from each school of thought seem to agree that environmental factors contribute to a homosexual orientation. The contributing factors that are most often identified are:[4]

- General conditioning and learning
- Parental and family conditioning
- Desire to accept the role of the other sex
- Real dangers and difficulties of heterosexuality
- Need to be loved
- Secondary gain
- Antisexuality and puritanism
- Fixation and fetishism
- Inadequacy feelings
- Hostility and rebelliousness
- Severe emotional difficulties

In addition to and in combination with those factors is personal choice. A child who is in the process of developing a sexual orientation may choose to respond positively or negatively to his father, mother, or peer group. He may choose to participate or withdraw from activities with the same sex or the other sex. As the child matures he may choose to participate or withdraw from sexual activities with others of the same sex. The choices continue: to visualize and think about homosexual activity, or not to do so; to accept the label of homosexual, or to struggle with homosexual feelings; as an adult, to choose a homosexual life-style or to discover a heterosexual life-style.

Evangelical Christians typically label homosexuality as the greatest sexual perversion known to man. It is seen as a sinful choice of behavior. Within many churches, there is a misconception that all homosexuality can be changed through spiritual conversion or by people trying harder to change. Those who are not willing to "try harder" are often isolated from the mainstream of fellowship.

It would be impossible to explore the subject of homosexuality in one book, let alone one chapter. There are plenty of resources on the topic, and we encourage mothers to read elsewhere. The purpose of this chapter is to alert mothers to the early warning signs of prehomosexual behavior in their sons and faulty parenting patterns that can influence a boy toward homosexual responses. The proper time for parents to become aware of these behaviors, and to counteract them, is between the ages of three and ten, long before children engage in activities that deserve to be called homosexual. There is agreement among experts that the earlier these tendencies are spotted, the more easily they are reversed.

I must make something clear from the beginning. If a mother detects these signals in her son, it does *not* mean her son will automatically become homosexual. Dr. Wardell B. Pomeroy, academic dean for the advanced study of human sexuality, says that a high percentage of boys have some kind of homosexual contact when they are growing up, and no homosexual contact in adult life.[5] Please, do not jump to conclusions. Rather, be aware, investigate, and then discuss your findings with an objective friend or professional.

Mental health experts suggest that homosexual signs are visible early in the vast majority of boys. The pattern of behavior is now fairly clear. Most of these boys tend to be overpolite, obedient, anxious to please adults, charming, witty, and cute. They are excessively fearful of physical injury in childhood. Out of 106 homosexual case studies, 89 of the boys avoided physical fights, 60 were isolated loners, and only 7 were involved in competitive group games.[6]

Prehomosexual children also tend to isolate themselves. This leads to other children teasing and labeling them as different. Many homosexual men feel they were alienated as early as they can remember. They say other kids, particularly boys, were mean to them when they were children. One man said, "I lived most of my life terrified of my homosexual feelings. When I was six or seven I realized that my feelings about other boys weren't normal. I was bookish, not athletic. From the time I was in third grade, children called me a fairy. . . ."[7]

Sometimes a child with a homosexual orientation will develop a close relationship with another loner who has similar interests. If this happens, it's wise that parents ask the following questions:

- Are the boys involved with each other to the exclusion of others?
- Do they disappear to lonely places often?
- Are they excessively unhappy when separated?
- Do they show no interest in sports or other competitive activities?

If a little boy does not receive the love and affection he needs at home, there is a chance he will look for it elsewhere. He may develop an intense personal attraction to a male stranger.

Some prehomosexual boys are overly attached to and affectionate with their mothers and detached from their fathers. I remember a woman telling me, "My son is so mushy. He constantly wants to snuggle on my lap and fondle my breasts." Her son said, "My father is narrow-minded, mean, and old-fashioned. But my mom is broad-minded and modern. I love to hug and kiss Mom, even though it gets on her nerves, but I hate being around my dad. He is repulsive."[8] This is not normal behavior, especially for boys, six to eleven.

Most young boys are fascinated with the anatomy and functional capacity of the male organs. Prehomosexual boys tend to be sexually precocious and to develop sexual fantasies. They usually don't need a partner, but gratify themselves through masturbation. These associations amount to an eroticism which is ready to extend itself to a male partner. Maleness itself is the target.

Dr. C. A. Tripp's exhaustive book, *The Homosexual Matrix*, says that males who have a high homosexual proclivity often come from a sexually precocious segment of the population. They tend to arrive at puberty sooner and masturbate earlier and more extensively through their lives than males who mature later and are less sexually active.[9]

Faulty Fathering

Kevin was a nine-year-old boy whom everyone called "little shrimp." His father, Don, was a passive individual who had not worked a regular job for years. He spent most of his time away from home and neglected Kevin and his five brothers and sisters. Kevin and his mother came in to see me just after she divorced Don.

Kevin was very upset over the divorce. I was confused over his despair because he rarely saw his father before the split. Only twice in the last eighteen years had Don been home for Christmas dinner. With tears streaming down his face, Kevin explained.

"Dad played with us when he was home. We never have any fun with Mom because she's always worried about something."

His poor mother was left to support five children on welfare. She had good reason to worry.

"Kevin, I'm very sorry about your parents' divorce," I replied. "The welfare system is going to help you and your family now, and maybe your mom won't be as worried as before. That will make life easier on you, too."

Protesting through his sobs, he cried, "But now I will *never* have anyone to take me fishing or help me catch a ball."

I finally caught on. Kevin was telling me he was afraid of becoming a male adult. As long as he knew his father was remotely connected with him, he hung onto his fantasy that one day his father would come home and help him grow up. He probably didn't miss his particular father, but he did miss *a* father, *a* man, and *a* male to help him survive as a boy.

I knew Kevin was very vulnerable, so I hunted for a suitable and sympathetic church that would be willing to help this poor family and provide surrogate fathers. A local Presbyterian congregation opened their arms to them and by the end of the year, Kevin and his brother had become Christians. The wonderful male Sunday school teachers acted as father substitutes for them.

It's a crime that so many fathers are absent when their sons are growing up. The implications are sobering. Prehomosexual boys say their relationships with their fathers are characterized by distance, antagonism, fear, and mutual low regard. In a study of 106 homosexual adults, 79 of the men reported having fathers who were detached from them.[10] Psychiatrists say they rarely see a homosexual who has had a good relationship with his father. But, for fathers who are a positive influence on their sons, there is good news. Recent research seems to indicate that *fathers have an absolute veto power over homosexual development in their sons.*[11]

A father-son relationship characterized by warmth, affection, and mutual respect lays the groundwork for a boy to feel comfortable with his father and other men. A close relationship with Dad can boost a boy's self-esteem and help him feel relatively certain about his masculine identity and unthreatened in other relationships.[12]

Unfortunately, loving father-son relationships don't exist in every home. Some fathers want a masculine, athletic son and are disappointed when they don't get one. Numerous times I've seen little boys rejected because they didn't measure up to their fathers' expectations of "manliness." One adult who grew up under these conditions said, "I always felt that social acceptance depended on athletic prowess. To flub was to be excluded from society, or at the very least ridiculed. Because I was a dud on the playing field, I strove to prove I was a man in every possible way. My father called me a sissy. He wanted me to play like a real boy . . . eventually the rift between us widened. He was cold toward me, refusing to attend my graduation from high school, college, or medical school. This silent hostile man became a specter that haunted me for years."[13]

While some fathers withdraw, others are simply too physically rough with their sons in the early years. Consequently, their little boys become afraid of them and tend to cling to their mothers. Emotional tough talk doesn't help, either. I've seen fathers tease and ridicule their sons, trying to shame them into being more masculine. This is damaging to a boy who is in the process of forming his identity. The crass remarks hurt deeply, especially when affection is rarely shown in the home.

On the opposite end of the spectrum from the ultramasculine father who demands too much is the wishy-washy weakling who expects nothing from his son. This type of individual is inadequate as a husband and father. He generally leaves all parenting responsibilities to his wife and passively watches life happen around him. He doesn't bother to insist on anything from his children, and he avoids all types of hassles. Consequently he wins favor from his kids, and Mom is viewed as the strict, hard-headed disciplinarian.

It's fairly common for a passive man to try to undermine his wife's disciplinary actions. When she objects to his tactics, the kids usually think she is a bully. Playing the game out to its finish, he is likely to say politely, "Just do what your mother wishes." What he really means is, "I really would like to help you, but your mother will throw a fit if I don't go along with her. You know how she is!"

An overprotective father can also cause problems for his son in later life. This type of father rushes to school to bully a teacher when his child gets into trouble, or rescues him from the negative consequences of his actions. Over-protective fathers are, in the long run, doing a disservice to their children.

Faulty Mothering

I'd like to make something very clear: I am not trying to condemn anyone or point a finger at good mothers and bad mothers. I simply want to identify various types of faulty mothering patterns that may influence a child toward homosexual-type behavior. The first faulty pattern is overly permissive mothering.

I once asked a young mother if she would like to go with me and a group of other women to a conference. At first, I hesitated to ask, because I knew she was a single mother with three children.

"I know this is a last-minute invitation. Do you think you can make arrangements for your children on such short notice?" I asked.

"Oh, sure!" she replied. "The kids are old enough to

take care of themselves. I'll give them money for hamburgers and they can ride their bikes or watch TV and play. They'll love a day to themselves."

"I can't guarantee when we will be home, because some of the women might want to have supper at a restaurant after the conference," I warned.

"Oh, my kids can manage very easily. I don't worry about what they do anymore. I have to trust them because I can't be everywhere at once."

Her responses startled me. In an age when more and more children are reported missing, mothers must make sure their children are well supervised. There is a fine line between permissiveness and neglect, and in my opinion, she was teetering between the two.

Permissive mothers try to buy love by begging their children to cooperate and not saying no to their requests. This rarely works, because boys don't easily give up when they want something. I remember watching a boy in my office try thirteen times during the hour to get what he wanted. Finally his poor mother said, "See how he is? He never gives up!"

"May I handle this?" I said carefully.

After she nodded, I got down on the floor, looked at her little rascal in the eyes, and said, "I will not let you do this. I'm bigger, and I will not change my mind. If you try to do this again, I will hold you and stop you from doing it."

My voice was low, with a deadly tone of authority. I wanted him to know I would not compromise and I was in control. He made one more weak effort to get his way, while keeping an eye on my every move. I inched closer. Suddenly he burst into tears and ran to his mother. After this, the trouble stopped. I cannot say this strongly enough. Mothers need to be tough, regardless of whether or not they have a strong husband around.

When a mother is excessively permissive and father is more stern, the kids will see her as a good guy, and Dad will be thrust into a bad-guy role. The kids may jump to the conclusion that Mom is on their side no matter what they do. This can be detrimental to little boys, because they are likely to overidentify with their weak mother.

Women must guard against this kind of mothering. The world we live in drives a hard bargain in the business of giving and taking. Permissiveness may produce a spoiled, demanding child, who as an adult lives out the same tactics and is shoved aside by others.

The overprotective mother can create other problems for her son, too. This type of mother shields her children from all threatening situations and danger. As far as she is concerned, rough sports and rambunctious peers are a no-no. Her children are kept close to her side so she can guard them at all times. She believes, "No one can give my children what they need the way I can."

When her children get into trouble, she runs to their rescue and doesn't allow them to face situations themselves. Maneuvering to control, she uses every excuse imaginable: "They provoked him to do it. . . . They set him up. . . . He didn't understand he was doing damage. . . . You always use him as a scapegoat. . . . He was only defending himself. . . . My child said he didn't do it, and he never lies." Believe me, I've heard them all.

When Dad steps in to discipline his son, the overprotective mother gets in the middle to shield him from a firm hand. This is unfortunate, because a little boy needs his father's masculine training and discipline. Consequently, the boy becomes more bold in his naughtiness because he never pays the consequences for his misdeeds. Since Mom constantly lets him off the hook, he thinks, "I can get away with doing whatever I want."

In his book, *Their Mother's Sons*, Edward Strecker, a consultant to the secretary of war and surgeon general of the army, air force, and navy, makes an impassioned appeal to American mothers who spoil and overprotect their sons. He begs them to wake up and stop producing immature sons who are tied to their mother's apron strings: "It is a danger to our democratic civilization and culture to keep children entombed psychologically and not permit them to grow up emotionally and socially. It is a grave menace. Over protected male children tend to be immature throughout life."[14]

Indulgent mothers go one step beyond the overprotective mother. They not only let children do what they want, they also give them too much and make too many sacrifices for them. They buy them the best brands of clothing, excuse them from earning money, and regularly hand out five-dollar bills. They rarely make their children do anything around the house, but typically wait on them hand and foot. They clean the bedrooms and pick up scattered toys while saying, "There is plenty of time for teaching my son responsibility. He's my baby, and I just hate to see him grow up so fast. I want him to enjoy his childhood as long as possible."

If only the indulgent mother could realize her silver cords are too tight. She's teaching her son to be overly dependent and hindering his development in the process.

One study reported that homosexual men had unusually close relationships with their mothers. They were babied through childhood. Their mothers were excessively affectionate and fostered an undue dependency in them. Because Mom was overprotective and indulgent, this made her much easier for the little boy to cope with than Dad. Her type of mothering seemed to whittle down the chances of the father being a strong male model to his son.

Overdependence on Mom after the latency years is harmful. I've noticed that boys during junior high often act cruelly and hatefully toward their mothers. Periodically they are cold and distant. I wonder if some of these children are struggling to establish their autonomy. Perhaps boys with overindulgent mothers feel they are being strangled emotionally, and therefore fight for space. I suggest there is a link between a boy's obstinate behavior and his mother's doting behavior.

Experts agree that there is nothing stronger in the world than the mother-child bond. But this cohesion must be cultivated with wisdom. A smart mother isn't overprotective or indulgent. She assists her children to stand on their own feet.

Some theorize that cold, emotionally aloof mothers can also contribute to the development of homosexual-type behavior in their sons. These mothers don't express affection and do little to meet their children's emotional needs. In many cases they are women who don't like being mothers and have many unmet needs themselves.

A homosexual adult who was raised with a cold, unapproachable mother said, "No matter how hard I tried to get my mother to love me, she wouldn't. As I got older it was easier to hate her, than to try to win her over. . . . Women are like that. . . . I don't want anything to do with them."

This particular homosexual was angry toward his mother and unable to see that all women aren't like her. His hatred spread to all females, and he turned to men for friends and lovers.

Raising a sexually secure boy requires care and attention from Mom. When a home has a warm and loving atmosphere, sexual hang-ups are less likely to develop. Parents do their children a favor by expressing affection to them and to each other in appropriate ways.

Some mothers have difficulty showing affection because they didn't receive it when they were growing up. Even though they may feel love for their families, they may not be able to express it physically. You have probably heard the expression "You learn how to do something by doing it." Just because a mother didn't learn how to give and receive affection during childhood doesn't mean she can't learn as an adult. A touch of a hand or an arm around her son's shoulder is a way to start. Eventually she can aim toward giving hugs.

There are instances when a boy may suffer because his mother is too frantically busy to meet his needs. Unfortunately, in today's society this is a universal problem. There are numerous places where women can spend their time and energies. This is particularly true if a woman is talented and inclined to be successful in whatever she does.

I must speak to this issue. As mothers and wives, we must ration our physical, emotional, and psychic energies. We are not omnipotent. We cannot be spread in one hundred different directions and function well.

I cannot count the number of husbands I have talked with who are exasperated about their wives' overcommitment to church activities. They are lonely because their wives are always at some kind of church function. They are angry because their wives say, "So-and-so needed my attention." Their response is, "Well, what about me and the kids? We need your attention, too!"

It isn't easy balancing the roles of wife, mother, professional, and minister. My husband and I came to America to be full-time Christian workers when our children were six, nine, and twelve years old. We loved our Christian tasks, but had to work very long hours. The children were with us all the time, but as I reflect back on those years, I now feel they were neglected. We were too busy and our energies were flowing into our work, instead of into our kids. Our children will tell you that they enjoyed living on a Christian campus all the time, but I do not feel it was good for them to have only a part of my life. I was too involved in a Christian career at a crucial time in their lives. I worry over this at times, but then my kids worry over me because I'm worrying, so I'm trying to forgive myself for my faulty mothering pattern.

Today I encourage myself and other parents to evaluate

their time commitments outside the home. What involvements are absolutely necessary? Can some commitments wait until another time in life? Time schedules need assessment. Activities need appraisals. Parents need to ask: Do my commitments match my priorities?

Another type of mother who is in charge of raising homosexual boys is the mother who dominates the family. In a study of 106 homosexuals, 81 had dominating mothers.[15] These women were the chief authority figures in their homes.

Children tend to identify most with whoever holds the most powerful position in their lives. If a boy perceives his mother to be the more effective, more powerful, and more attractive parent, he may be likely to identify more with his mother than his father.

I can see the single mother throwing up her hands and saying, "Well, where does that put me? I'm the only parent my son has!" All mothers, with or without husbands, can choose whether they will lead their children or dominate them. There is a difference.

A dominating mother talks all the time and does not listen to what her children try to tell her. She chops off their comments before they are finished and rushes into giving answers and directions before all the facts are collected. She tells others what to do, gives advice before others ask for it, and acts as if she knows more than others around her. In most cases is very organized and efficient in performing tasks, but she railroads people in the process.

A mother who leads her children takes time to listen to their thoughts and feelings. She doesn't pretend to have all the answers, and she avoids jumping to conclusions. When her children ask for help, she is willing to assist them, but her goal is to help them learn, not to do everything for them.

All Children Are Unique

Children are born very different from one another. A story told by a psychiatrist beautifully illustrates this point. During his early training in California, he assisted many families at a county mental health center. One of the families he worked with was quite interesting.

The family lived on several acres and worked the land for food. The father was also on a road construction crew that moved about the state according to job demands. He was rarely home during the week but always returned on weekends. Though he was gone most of the time, everyone knew he was the master of the family. His wife and children were expected to abide by his strict rules and to accomplish all the farm chores. When he returned, his wife gave him detailed reports about the week. Any tiny infraction of his rules meant punishment. As immigrants from Europe, these parents felt it was absolutely necessary to work hard in order to get ahead. The children had little time for play between their schoolwork and chores.

At the time the young doctor was involved with this family, all of the children were adults. One boy had become a famous millionaire. Two other children married and settled out in the country, living ordinary family lives. The other two adults were schizophrenics unable to function in everyday life.[16]

All of the children were raised under similar conditions, yet they were all different as adults. I know of other cases where sons raised in the same home turned out to have different sexual life-styles.

It's hard to answer the question "Why?" Perhaps they started out different at birth and were treated the same by their parents. Maybe the parents responded differently to each child, so that a variety of environments were set up inside the home. It's possible that strong peer influences swayed them from what they had been taught at home. We will probably never know the precise answer. But the point is that all children are different and must be handled according to their God-given temperament and predisposition.

Thinking It Through

1. What are some of the signs of prehomosexual behavior?

2. Explain two faulty fathering patterns.

3. How does the overly permissive mother act? The overprotective mother? The overindulgent mother? The dominating mother?

4. If a mother sees herself leaning toward a faulty mothering pattern, what can she do to help herself move away from that pattern?

5. Evaluate your time commitments. Do you feel impressed to make any changes?

6. Define the unique characteristics of each of your children.

7. What have you learned from this chapter that you can share with one other mother this week? When and with whom will you do this?

7

Take the Whining
Out of Work _____ ▪

I grew up in a beautiful subtropical town where my
dad was the head of an agricultural school. He was
wonderful with boys and taught the young men to love
work. He managed his four children the same way he
did his schoolboys, and also taught us to enjoy hard
work.

I vividly remember an incident that happened one
Saturday morning during my childhood. The day was
blazing hot. Most folks determined to accomplish their
tasks before midday. As we were finishing breakfast,
Daddy peered out the kitchen window and said, "Whew!
It's going to be another beast of a day. The weather is
much too hot for children to go out in the garden. I'll go
out and hoe the vegetables alone. This job must be done
today." Then, with a gleam in his eye, he said, "Children
aren't tough enough for this job. You stay in the cool
house; I'll do it alone!"

In protest we said, "We're tough, Daddy! We aren't
sissies in the heat!"

"No, no, children," he argued. "I cannot let you help
me today." Glancing out the window again, he lowered

his voice. "What a shame. I hate hoeing alone on Saturdays!"

"But Daddy, we want to go with you!" we exclaimed. With a hint of surrender in his voice, he warned, "It's a scorching sunburn kind of a day." We pleaded and assured him that we liked suntans. A funny smirk crossed his face, and he finally gave in to our begging. "Well, perhaps you can join me in the garden, but all of you must put your sun hats on first."

Father was not dumb. He knew exactly how we would respond, having done this many times before. Now, follow me into the garden.

It was blistering hot, and all of us perspired heavily. Daddy gave us each a long, wide row to hoe, and he hoed the middle row in between us. A minute didn't pass without him coaching us: "You children are great. I want to let you in on a secret: I never worked like you when I was your age. I dodged these jobs and left your two uncles to do it all. I liked to slip away and shoot rabbits instead!" (Grandmother Hilton said he stretched the truth. He really worked very hard as a child.)

"Do we really work better than you did, Daddy?" we asked.

His encouragement continued: "You children are great little workers. My goodness, my hoe bumped something, but I can't find it. Would someone come over here and look around where I've been working?"

Hunting around a thick tangle of peas on pruned branches, my brother Murray suddenly blurted out, "Wow! I found a big cold bottle of lemonade! How did this get here? Dad, Dad, can we have this?"

"Goodness me," Daddy replied, "I have no idea how this got here. But I brought the garden mugs, so why don't we all sit down near the big fig tree and take a rest?"

After our thirst was quenched, we finished raking the vegetable patch while Father commented on the way we handled our hoes, taking time to teach each of us. We never knew we were being taught, because Dad made learning a happy experience. We probably did a lousy job completing work assignments now and then, but he never said we performed poorly. He always found something good to commend and showed us how to make improvements.

With a full morning of work behind us, we followed Daddy into the house. As he walked through the front door, his words echoed through every room. "Edith, where are you? I have a fine band of workers here, and we're all hungry. These children are great helpers. I could never have managed on my own." By now we were red faced and wilted, but we felt like Australian pioneers, proud of our accomplishments.

The Wicked Witch of the West

Daddy was an expert in getting us to do our chores. But many Moms feel helpless in this area. All their efforts to motivate children to work end in big, fat fights.

"Billy is here, Mom. Can I go to his house to play?" Johnny asks.

"Have you finished emptying the wastepaper baskets and straightening your room?" calls his mom.

"Do I have to?" howls Johnny. "I get all the lousy jobs around this dump! Billy isn't a slave at his house!"

Johnny's mother is nearly ready to resign from motherhood. "Why, oh, why does he put me through this in front of his friends? I feel like the Wicked Witch of the West. I can't understand why his friends never have to do chores," she mutters to herself.

Actually most of Johnny's friends are required to do odd jobs, but boys rarely publicize helping Mom around the house. They might brag about working with Dad because there's something impressive about doing masculine work, but helping Mom is often kept secret.

Getting children to do their chores is an uphill battle for

most mothers because they prefer being peacemakers and don't like to bicker. Conflict makes them feel inadequate. They assume other families have more responsible children who always follow through with their duties. This is a fantasy.

When I was raising my children, I struggled with these thoughts and feelings. Battling with David used to exhaust me. He had a will of iron and actually enjoyed making me upset. When he was older, he confessed that he felt powerful when he provoked me to the boiling point. Each time he succeeded, he calmly chalked up another victory for himself. Even if he didn't win an argument, he still felt superior because he had exasperated me. Once he boasted, "I can make you mad anytime I choose. Poor old Mum!"

I shall never forget listening to the lectures given by Dr. Harvey Kaufman, a famous child psychiatrist. He loved to shock his students into remembering his most important points. During one class he said: "A boy achieves his male maturity over his mother's dead body."

Any mother with a strong-willed son will discover this very, very early. She feels as if she is being constantly pulled into battle, even though she tries desperately to be a nice, calm mother who makes reasonable requests.

Many mothers love their sons, but when pressed to their limits, they explode in anger. Tremendous guilt follows on the heels of these outbursts. Feeling a need to be punished for yelling at her son, she may give up and retreat. This leaves the child feeling more powerful than ever.

Chores often evoke hassles with little boys because they feel that helping around the house is girls' work. They see the world on a male-female axis. I remember telling my four-year-old grandson, Michael, to pick up the magazines that were scattered on the floor. He looked at me with his hands on his hips and said, "Is that a girl fing or a boy fing? I won't do girl fings!" I know it sounds farfetched, but it isn't uncommon for little boys who grow up without a close male model to become preoccupied with these issues.

Contests over chores also happen when kids tire of routines (even though they need them). Even pleasant tasks, when done repetitively, become wearisome to most of us. We build up a natural resistance to the same old routine and try to find a way of escape.

I've also seen children use chores as leverage to manipulate their mothers. Brian said, "I miss my dad. He always used to take me fun places. You're a grouch. All you ever want me to do is go to school and do my chores."

Brian's mother feared she might lose her son's love to his glamorous father who was about to marry another woman. Since Brian was an only son, she thought her ex-husband would try to persuade Brian to live with him. She let Brian off the hook. Rather than making him do his chores, she gave him more free time to play. Brian won the war and mastered the art of manipulation. By the way, Brian's father was never interested in having Brian live with him and his new wife.

The fact is that many boys enjoy striving. It feels good to challenge and defy their all-important mother. With some children, this begins at birth.

So what is a mother to do? How can she alleviate some of her own frustrations and help promote a cease-fire with her kids? Here are some tips that help many mothers maintain their equilibrium when their kids try to knock them off balance.

Supervision Brings Satisfaction

There is a misconception in American culture today that women with children must be supermoms. The thought is ridiculous. Women with children don't need to be supermoms, but they do need to be supervisors. The good news is that any ordinary mother can be a supervisor.

What is a supervisor? Let's look at the Latin roots of the word. *Super* means "over," and *visor* comes from "videre," meaning "to see." A supervisor is simply one who oversees.

I've heard many frustrated mothers say, "My son is not a self-starter. I cannot get him to follow through with his chores."

I remember a conversation I had with an exasperated mother who was very upset because she had to nag her son to do his chores. Her husband was gone most of the time on business, so he couldn't help solve the problem.

"What does your husband do at his firm?" I asked.

"Carl is a manager on his floor."

"Do the people in his department all do exactly what they are supposed to do?"

"Few of them work to full capacity if Carl relaxes his efforts."

"Why? They are trained adults and know how to be responsible, don't they?"

"I never thought about that, but I know Carl works very hard, looking after them."

"Does your husband answer to someone above him?"

"Yes. Once a week, he meets with his boss, who supervises the supervisors."

After a few moments of silence, she said, "Now I see. Everyone must answer to someone. Even the president of his company is accountable to the board of directors."

In our society we associate many functions with the job of a supervisor. Managing, teaching, instructing, and enforcing rules are a few of the duties involved. A supervisor holds people accountable, motivates, inspires, and sets time limits for a particular piece of work. He does everything he can to help his workers achieve their maximum potential.

A mother is no different. If she wants her children to clean the dining table efficiently and wash the dishes, she must give them specific guidelines and instruction. Then she must oversee the process until the kids have the system down pat. Only at this point is intermittent rather than constant supervision needed. One word of caution: When you diminish the amount of direct observation, don't let up on giving encouragement. Praise keeps children motivated to continue their efforts and helps them feel good about themselves.

Jobs can be designed according to the age of children. Children of two and three are capable of carrying their plates and silverware to the kitchen. Four- and five-year-olds can clear the table and scrape dishes before they are washed. Older children can wrap leftovers and load and unload the dishwasher. With a little planning, everyone can pitch in and help. (For a detailed list of jobs that children in various age groups are able to accomplish, *see* Appendix 2.)

"But I feel like a perpetual *nag*, like I'm always a bad guy!" some complain. May I make a suggestion? Try to think of yourself in a different way. Try to see yourself as the person God has placed in your home to be a supervisor. Be creative playing this role.

For many years our family had an imaginary servant called Bridget. We always joked about Bridget's terrible laziness. When there was work to be done around the house, I usually grabbed the grandchildren's attention by talking about Bridget.

"Children, I expected Bridget to be back tonight, but I guess she got lazy again. One of these days I'm going to have to fire her. I see no sign of her at all, and I really need her help, because this house is a mess. Oh dear, what am I going to do?"

"Nana, Bridget is awful. She's never here when you need her!" the children replied.

"Sometimes she does good work, but I just don't know what I'm going to do tonight. I really need help."

"Maybe we could all help, Nana."

"That would be wonderful! You always do a much

better job than Bridget, anyway. Now, who will be the first to volunteer?"

The grandchildren had great fun pretending with me, and they took pride in knowing they worked better than Bridget. After they began working, I told them stories about my childhood. They loved hearing tales about my mischievousness. But they were even more delighted to hear stories about the naughty things their parents did. Of course, most of these were censored, so they wouldn't get any bright ideas for misbehaving from dear old Nana. I saved these stories as a treat for when they were helping me, to take their minds off the toil of their labors.

Inspection

It's Saturday morning, and Matthew is about to run out of the house to play. "Mom, I've finished my room. Can I go now?" he yells, leaping through the front door.

"Okay, I'm glad you did your jobs," calls Mom from the kitchen. Matthew didn't hear a word she said. He was already out of sight in the neighbor's backyard.

Later, Matthew's mother takes an armful of clean clothes into his room. The bedspread is pulled over an unmade bed, and his dirty underclothes are kicked under the covers along with several pairs of dirty socks. The radio is on, the desk lamp and overhead light are burning brightly, and his homework hasn't been touched. Mom is fuming and ready to throw the clean clothes in the trash and torch the place.

Many little boys are eager to finish a job quickly so they can watch TV or play with neighborhood friends. Sloppiness and parental anger result when chores aren't inspected. One of the most important jobs a mother has as a supervisor is to make a final check of her children's work. Inspection is a boring job for Mom, and sometimes it means conflict when her kids are careless about their duties. Nevertheless, it must be done to teach children efficiency.

Matthew's mother and I discussed her household frustrations, and she left my office with a battle plan. She handled Matthew differently the following week.

The familiar scenario began as usual. "I finished my room, Mom. I'm going out to play now. No homework this week."

"Not so fast, young man. I'm going to inspect your room, first. You are not to run off until I check the job with you."

Well aware of the mess in his room, Matthew hesitated and mumbled, "Maybe I forgot to do a few things."

"Let's go see how you did," his mother responded as she led him down the hall to his room. Pulling the crumpled bed apart, she instructed, "Matthew, I will work with you and we will make the bed together this time. Next time I want you to do it the way I show you, and you are not to leave this house until I am satisfied with what you've done."

Matthew soon learned that he couldn't dupe his mother any longer, and eventually he met her standards, which were tailored to his age and abilities. Even though consistent inspection was hard work, Matthew's mother agreed it was easier than dealing with the anger his sloppiness sparked when he wasn't supervised.

Some pressure is taken off Mom if she makes inspection time fun. Humor is helpful. You need not rule with an iron fist. Children learn best when they're having a good time. Perhaps you might try the white-glove approach with a foreign accent.

My children loved to play an inspection game with me when they were young. We pretended that a very famous person was going to come to visit. The girls loved imagining a lord and lady coming from their castle. First the children acted like the famous guest. They went outside, walked in the front door to our messy house, and then imitated what the famous people would do when they saw everything topsy-turvy. You should have seen how they tried to outdo each other with their dramatic reactions! It was quite comical. We went from one room to the next discovering messes, dramatizing, and then putting things in order, the way a lord and lady would prefer to see things.

I realize that work is not always going to be fun for children and parents. There is no magic solution for getting boys to cooperate, and a mother won't always be able to make her children work without some feelings of exasperation. Many boys go to battle when you mention the word *work*. But, perhaps some of these suggestions can prevent an escalation of war.

Through the years I have passed on to others the things Daddy taught me, and I've repeatedly seen his methods work. Rambunctious children, grandchildren, and an entire dormitory of teenage girls became productive as they were guided toward discovering the fun hidden in their labors. Creative supervision was the key that unlocked the door to those discoveries, and to my sanity as an overseer.

A Cushioned Retreat?

A psychologist once asked me, "Jean, why are chores an essential part of a boy's upbringing? Aren't their studies, music lessons, and baseball practices enough?"

I maintain that boys must be required to do chores for several reasons. When they are responsible for household duties, they learn to contribute to the family as a team member. This type of cooperation teaches them to be other-centered. If all their activities are fun involvements focused strictly on their own interests, they're likely to become self-centered. Routine jobs build character and teach children to be responsible to loved ones.

For many years as a family therapist, I counseled

numerous unemployed men with families. It was routine for me to explore their backgrounds. Despite many job opportunities, these men couldn't hold a job. Even when they liked a particular kind of work, inevitably something went wrong and they were unemployed again. In all these cases, I consistently saw one common denominator: These men were never required to work around the house when they were growing up. They were never taught to responsibly and efficiently complete a chore. A portion of the men grew up with adult supervision virtually absent. Some had mothers who waited on them hand and foot. Others were sickly and excused from overexertion. Often their single mothers labored long hours and were too fatigued to teach them work-related skills. Some simply considered their home a cushioned retreat for their children.

One mother told me: "I believe in pampering my kids after school. I require as little as possible after they have had a full day of studies."

"With your husband away most of the time, don't you need some help from them around the house?" I inquired.

"I suppose that would be nice. But I came from such an unhappy home that I want to make theirs as peaceful as possible. I made a decision when my first son was born that my kids would enjoy their childhood. I want to give them all the happiness I can while they are young."

Unfortunately Carol's plan was not working. Her boys were not happy or appreciative. That's why she sought counseling. She continued: "My boys seem depressed and bored, and their quarreling is driving me crazy. I don't ever remember fighting with my brothers and sisters like they do. You'd think they hate each other. I never had time to bicker like them. My parents always had us busy working on one odd job after another."

The lights went on for Carol. She had just solved her own dilemma. By not teaching her sons to work for the good of the family, Carol was encouraging laziness, immaturity, and selfishness—the perfect ingredients for producing sibling battles. Carol assumed that lots of play meant lots of happiness. She overcompensated for her disappointments during childhood and tried to act out her own childhood fantasies through her children. But her boys were unhappy and restless because they had no challenges or contrasts in their lives.

As we talked, Carol began to see the importance of balancing work and play. She desperately wanted her sons to be happy, and soon realized that happiness cannot be a goal in itself. Happiness is the by-product of duty well-done. Without work, Carol's boys were robbed of happiness.

I could empathize with Carol because I ran into the same problem with my children when they were very young. We had moved to a beautiful rural area to live in a very old stone house nestled in an orchard of nut and fruit trees. Lyall and I thought this would be an ideal setting for raising our young family. With a long summer vacation ahead, we were certain the children would have great fun playing in the big open spaces of our land.

It didn't take long for us to realize that our dreams of a perfect summer were crumbling. The children grew tired of playing and kept complaining, "We're bored! There's nothing to do around here!" The neighborhood children came and went while I played referee, settling disputes and watching for mischief. Then it dawned on me: Play alone was not providing enough structure for them. No wonder they were restless and quarrelsome. I set out to change things, stepped onto my soapbox, and declared to my kids: "I am fed up with what is happening around here, and things are going to change. From now on, our mornings are going to be quite different."

David, my eight-year-old, broke in, "We don't want any changes 'cept to go to the zoo more."

I became more direct in my explanation: "David, your quarreling with the other boys in the neighborhood is terrible, and there must be a change in your behavior. We will do jobs every morning, and there will be no kids in our yard during that time. You may play in the afternoon, if your chores are done and your bedroom is neat."

Disgusted with me, the children cried, "That's awful! Other mothers don't make their kids work in the summer!"

David protested even more vehemently, "What will we tell our friends when they want to play with us in the morning? I know. I'll tell them our mother is mean and cruel and she makes us work on our holidays," to which I replied, "I couldn't care less what you tell them. The rules remain."

My daughter Robin wondered if they would be paid for their work. Lyall and I had already decided that we would pay them for extra jobs outside their normal chores, but there would be no compensation for regular duties.

As it turned out, their vacation was wonderful. The children learned to care for their own little garden that first summer, and two of them sold their produce. David took care of the chickens and sold eggs to me.

Today all my children are grown, and they love to tell their own children about how they worked as kids. Gardening is still one of their favorite pastimes, and Robin is becoming a fuchsia specialist. It all started that hot afternoon when I decided our home was not going to be a cushioned retreat, but a place where my children would learn to work.

Perhaps you're wondering if the kids were upset and griped about my mandate. To my surprise they didn't complain for more than a few days. As their energies were directed toward learning new tasks, they enjoyed their work and took pride in doing it well. Believe me, we showered them with praise for their accomplishments.

Little boys must be taught to work efficiently and to be

productive in a competitive society. Their first boss is their mother. If she teaches them well, there is a good chance they'll be successful when they face the world on their own as adults.

Thinking It Through

1. Getting children to do chores is often an uphill battle. What tactics do you use in your home to help your children get their work done?

2. How can mothers teach their sons that housework isn't only for girls?

3. How do you supervise your children?

4. Read the Appendix that lists work responsibilities for children. Which chores have you used in your home?

5. How do you inspect your children's work? How could you add humor and make this time fun?

6. Should the home be a cushioned retreat? What do you think?

7. What odd jobs do you have your children do around the house? How do you reward their efforts?

8. If you were to encourage another mother with something you learned from this chapter, what would you say?

8

All They Do Is Fight! ▪▪

"Dan gets everything he wants. It's not fair! He goes more places, has more clothes, and Mom takes his side on everything. I hate it," Robert said with disgust.

"Why do you tease Dan so much?" I asked.

"Because he deserves it!"

"But it upsets your mother," I replied. "Can't you go out of your way to make peace with Dan? He has many problems, you know."

"I know. Mom always tells me that stuff. Dan is her pet, and I get blamed for everything," he complained.

"Does Dan tease you, too?"

"All the time! But no one ever sees him do it."

"What does he do?" I asked.

"He comes in my room, kicks my chair, and runs off. He's smart, and does it behind Mom's back."

"Do you tell your mother when this happens?"

"It wouldn't do any good. She'd just call me a whining tattletale and say, 'I don't want to hear it.'"

"What do you usually quarrel about?" I asked. Robert's response caught me completely off guard.

"Sometimes when we play rough, we get mad and end

up hurting each other. Other times I wake up in a bad mood. If Dan is happy, I'll pick a fight." I marveled that this boy of thirteen and a half actually understood his motives for quarreling.

Dan and Robert are brothers who are less than one year apart. Dan was born to a teenage mother and adopted at birth by Susan. A few months after the adoption, Susan conceived, and six months later she gave birth to Robert. Two years later, her beautiful daughter, Marie, was born. This little girl had the sunniest disposition of any child I've known. Wherever she went, people fell in love with her. A few years later, Susan became a single mother after a tragic divorce.

I have been in touch with this family since the boys were born. From the time Dan was eighteen months old, he was hyperactive and destructive beyond the norm. Physicians discovered he had minimal brain damage in three areas of his brain. Susan enrolled him in a special school designed to work with his handicaps, and today he is doing well in his studies and developing beautifully.

But all of this took a toll on Robert, the middle child. Dan's problems required Susan's special attention and protection. Intelligent and charming Marie upstaged Robert in whatever he did.

Marie was the star and Dan was the baby. Who was Robert? He seemed to fall through the cracks, and no one missed him. Quarreling was simply one way Robert acted out his feelings.

There are two sides to every story. When I had the chance to see Dan, I asked him why he quarreled with Robert.

"I quarrel with him because he bugs me all the time," Dan responded.

"How does he bug you?"

"He teases me and calls me stupid." (Robert has a very high IQ and is extremely intelligent. Dan does seem dumb to him.)

"What else?" I asked.

"The kids around the neighborhood call me cigar face." (The side of Dan's face was slightly injured during his birth.)

"Does Robert call you that, too?"

"No, but he's always taking my things in my room."

"Do you ever tell your mother about this?"

"All the time. But she just tells me to settle down and get away from him."

Though the two boys are close in age, they are very different. Dan is mechanically inclined, and his possessions are important to him. When he is aggravated, he explodes and acts out his anger in physical ways. Robert, however, is articulate and uses teasing as his deadly weapon. Poor Susan has her hands full.

What's the answer? First of all, I think it helps mothers to know that sibling rivalry is normal. Quarreling is to be expected, and is sometimes useful, since the stresses children go through with their siblings may give them resources they can use later in life.

There are siblings who don't fight. I don't think we can assume that this is strictly the product of skilled parenting, because many skilled parents have children who quarrel. Sometimes a family simply has quiet children who avoid conflict. There are also cases where violent parents produce children who are terrified of any form of trouble. The motto these children live by is "Peace at all costs."

Dr. James Dobson says that when women are asked, "What is the most irritating part of raising children?" the unanimous answer is "Sibling rivalry!" Most parents are deeply concerned about the bickering they hear between their kids. A great deal of energy goes into settling battles and trying to teach children to get along together. However, in most households, no amount of preaching will entirely solve the problem. Parents can lower their own anxieties by dropping the belief that good homes don't have quarrels. Show me a "good family," and I'll bet we'll find children who have their moments of war! I think the only way parents can insure no sibling fights is to confine themselves to having one child.

Some experts say that parents should stay completely out of their children's quarrels. Perhaps this works at times, but I'm not sure I agree with the concept across the board. When small and large children are involved in a squabble, there is good reason for a mother to mediate. The younger child doesn't have the strength of the older one and needs protection. Mothers who have children of varying ages at home need to be "all ears."

Quarreling usually doesn't happen without reason. There are definite purposes behind it. Every fight has three layers: the immediate cause of trouble; the struggle for status; and the underlying core of resentment built up from years of rivalry for possession of the parent.[1]

We see this in Dan and Robert's rivalry. When Robert took one of Dan's toys from his room, there was an immediate cause for trouble. As the two of them fought, each struggled to show who was in control and most powerful. Dan attacked physically; Robert used verbal barbs. Of course, all of this was within Susan's hearing. As soon as the fight began, they knew her attention was hooked.

Susan was usually wise to these tactics and let the boys settle matters between themselves. This was a good approach, since they were only six months apart in age. In most respects they were an even match for each other. By not rushing to the scene whenever they fought, she didn't reward the behavior she wanted stopped. Dan and Robert learned they couldn't get their mom's undivided attention by squabbling.

Quarrels and Quick Conclusions

Children who are allowed to make peace between themselves usually tend to be more just and fair than an outsider who hasn't seen the whole fight. Susan told me about a recent incident where she would have been better off letting the boys settle the squabble. They were playing a game in Robert's bedroom while Susan entertained friends in the living room. Donald, another thirteen-year-old, walked into the room. Each boy claims that Donald is his best friend. Trouble started immediately.

"Hey, Donald," Robert called, "come look at my comics."

Dan interrupted, "No! Let's finish our game first."

"I don't want to," Robert replied. "I want to show Donald my stuff."

Dan was furious. "That's not fair! I was winning, and now you walk off."

"We can play that game anytime. I want to talk to Donald," Robert replied.

"Well, why don't we start another game so Donald can play, too?" Dan asked.

"I don't want to play anymore. Besides, Donald came over to see what comics I would trade with him."

Dan boiled inside as Robert shoved him completely out of the picture. With a burst of anger, Dan kicked the game all over the floor, and Robert rushed out of the room and into Susan's group of friends, screaming, "Dan is making trouble for us! He is throwing all my things around. Mom, come stop him!"

Susan ran to Robert's room, saw the mess, and right in front of everyone, yelled, "Dan, how could you do this to your brother's room? You go to your room this minute and stay there the rest of the evening."

Outraged, Dan tore out of the house and down the street on his bicycle. There was Susan, her hands in the air, totally humiliated in front of her friends.

You and I know what had happened. Robert provoked Dan by deliberately abandoning the game. Dan tried to suggest all three boys participate, but Robert maneuvered Donald, pushing Dan out in the cold. Susan didn't know this. All she saw was the messy room. From that observation she assumed she had caught the culprit and concluded Dan had deliberately caused trouble. Dan was victimized and Robert came out looking squeaky clean in his mother's eyes.

We can pick up some important lessons from this incident. First of all, if Susan was going to get involved, she should have asked for the complete story before jumping to conclusions. Second, anytime children are playing together in threesomes, there is likely to be strain. Adults even report this happening among themselves. Perhaps parents are wise to avoid these situations altogether.

Some Siblings Don't Like Each Other

If children chronically quarrel, why have them play together? Why give them the chance to fight? Why not separate them? I've posed these ideas to mothers before, only to hear, "That's ridiculous. They're brothers, and they must get along."

The truth is that some siblings don't like each other. Maybe they have completely different interests or personalities. Just being in the presence of one may irritate the other. This is horrifying to an idealistic mother who thinks it's her job to make her kids love one another. She feels like a failure or that her Christian image is tarnished because her children fight.

Just because children are siblings doesn't mean they will automatically be good friends. It helps to keep a long-range view in mind. Sibling relationships tend to get better as time passes.

It's Okay to Have Bad Feelings

Children can be taught it's normal to have good and bad feelings toward family members. Encouraging siblings to tell each other when they are mad or happy may improve communication and prevent silent wars from lingering for days. But this kind of openness doesn't happen overnight. Many children find it difficult to discuss angry feelings. Their guilt over their anger ties their tongues. Parents must give children the right to talk about these unpleasant feelings and then consistently encourage them to do so.

A boy who lives in the shadow of achieving brothers and sisters often does not feel good about himself. He may tend to provoke other siblings because it gives him a sense of superiority. He may not be as smart, athletic, or good-looking as his brothers and sisters, but he can control his "enemies" by making them upset.

Parents are naturally drawn to self-assured children who have pleasant dispositions. But the less-confident, troubled child needs more of his parents' time. If he feels appreciated and loved, he'll be less likely to clamor for attention. Individual time alone with a parent can help him feel secure so he doesn't have to try to one-up his brothers and sisters. A forty-five minute weekly date with Mom or Dad can work wonders.

If children are having extreme difficulties tolerating one another, parents may need to explain the difference between actions and feelings. They can insist that children act respectfully toward one another regardless of their feelings. If a child acts unkindly by hitting, swearing, or name-calling, he should be required to apologize for his poor behavior. He must be responsible for his actions, whether his feelings change or not.

This can be taken one step further. You have heard the saying "Feelings follow actions." When we go out of our way to be kind to someone we don't like, our feelings tend to change in the process. At family gatherings, children can be prompted to share positive things they see or like about one another. This will help them appreciate the uniqueness of each individual.

Private Property: Hands Off!

Sandy came to talk to me about her sons. They fought constantly, and she was frightened they might seriously hurt each other. Most of their arguments were centered around their possessions.

"They always rip things off from each other. This week Peter, my eleven-year-old, wore his brother's sweater to school without asking permission. Mike, who is thirteen, was so angered he was thirsting for revenge."

"What did you do about the problem?" I asked.

"I gave Mike a lecture about sharing his things. He gets new clothes more often because he's growing more rapidly, and Peter doesn't have many sweaters."

My response surprised Sandy, but I had to speak the truth.

"Sandy, it looks to me as if you have indirectly given Peter an okay to steal Mike's things if he has a need. Is this really what you want to do?"

Sandy was a bit disgusted with me. "Don't you believe my boys should be taught to share with each other?"

My reply was pointed. "Sandy, this is not a matter of sharing. One boy is taking something that is not his. When sharing is negotiated by both boys, that's a different matter. Peter stole that sweater!"

I firmly believe that boys should not have to share their own special possessions. I've talked with many young people who say their moms scold them for being selfish if they get mad when someone takes something from their rooms. This is not fair to youngsters.

I suggest a complete ban on borrowing. Parents can prevent many quarrels by making a strict rule that someone else's property is off limits and no one touches another's belongings without permission.

Some Boys Like to Fight

Not all arguments are sponsored by differences. Some boys simply like to pick fights, especially if they're bored and have nothing better to do. My son, David, was an expert at this. He specialized in teasing his sisters and knew exactly how to provoke them. The rewards were wonderful for him: The girls became furious and exploded. He gloated over his slain victims and then innocently said, "How did I know she would get so mad over nothing?"

Some children are contentious by nature. Remember what Robert said earlier? He often picked fights with Dan just because he was in a bad mood and Dan was happy. Dan had done nothing to Robert. Robert was just mad at everything and demanded company in his misery.

I've seen many parents make the mistake of holding an older child responsible for all the upsets that happen between siblings. They say, "You are older. You know better, and we expect you to set a good example." Good examples are important, but sometimes younger children cause the conflicts. They resent the older child because he has more privileges and fewer restrictions. To get even, they act like a nuisance and then run screaming to Mommy when retaliation occurs. The baby of the family gets off the hook, and the older child gets stiff discipline. It's hardly fair.

As parents and grandparents, we must guard ourselves from making quick decisions about children who are quarreling. It's too easy to pounce on the child who upsets us most or overprotect another. The protected child will learn he has his mother wrapped around his finger and it's fun to cause trouble. Why not? Whenever he does, his siblings suffer and he gets off scot-free.

Don't Show Favoritism

You notice I said don't *show* it. It's common for parents to have special feelings for certain children, but they must not let those feelings show. The good, obedient child who tries hard to please his parents is very easy to love. He doesn't cause trouble, and his accomplishments bring great delight. The compliant child validates us and makes us feel we are good parents.

During my years in family counseling, I saw many cases where darling, well-behaved little girls got most of the attention in their family. When goodies were handed out, they were served first. The rambunctious boys had to wait. When mothers went on special outings such as shopping or to women's functions, it was easy for them to take along a little girl. The boys didn't seem to fit in the same way, so they got left with a baby-sitter. The boys resented this and sometimes picked fights with their sister to get even.

Hunger Spells Trouble

When my children were young, we lived in Australia, and they had a long walk home from school every day. We had no school buses, and the climate was hot. My stomach used to churn just before they were due home because I dreaded the quarreling that went on among them. Over the years I learned some simple tricks to keep peace in the house.

I learned it was best to keep short gaps between meals. The children were very hungry after school, so I fed them an early 5:00 P.M. dinner and sent them off to do their homework. My husband ate a peaceful meal an hour or so later, after arriving from work. When the children were done with their studies, he spent time with them.

When Lyall's work took him away for a few months at a time, I ate my supper early with the children and then we all had a snack before bed. There was a remarkable difference in all our attitudes after we had a good meal at the end of the day. I firmly believe that children develop a "biting" attitude when they are hungry, and they take it out on the family first.

I've also noticed that the dinner table can be a breeding

ground for quarrels as siblings strive to obtain their parents' attention. Parents do not have to put up with this at mealtime. There are better options. Either the parents can remove themselves from the table and leave the kids to eat alone, or they can dismiss the children until they are ready to stop fighting. Children need to hear their parents say, "We refuse to eat with you when you fight."

What Should I Do?

I'd like to close this chapter with some basic *do*s and *don't*s for parents who are worn-out by their kids' constant bickering. No one has a magic answer to this dilemma, but here is a summary of ideas that are known to help.

Please Don't!

- Don't feel guilty and condemn yourself because your children quarrel.
- Don't condemn yourself for being upset when your children quarrel. The most dedicated and caring mothers feel uneasy with tension in their homes.
- Don't assume you know who the troublemaker is in a fight. Sometimes children are simply incompatible. They "bug" each other, not by what they do, but simply by being in the same room together.
- "Don't make the oldest child responsible all the time. He can't be a perfect model all the time."[2]
- Don't overprotect your favorite child, or a sick child. One mother told me her healthy little girl said, "I wish I had asthma like my brother." The daughter had interpreted overprotection as favoritism, and this led to quarrels.
- "Don't allow older children to tease younger children, or younger children to harass older children."[3]
- "Don't ever compare siblings in their presence. This will set them up to fight. In the matter of beauty, brains, and

athletic ability, each child should know that in his parents' eyes, he is respected and has equal worth."[4]

• Don't allow long lapses between meals. Hunger can cause unnecessary problems.

Please Do!

• Do remember quarreling usually has multiple causes. There is more to a fight than what appears on the surface. Simple solutions may simply act like a bandage at times.
• Do separate children who quarrel. Nothing will be solved by forcing them to play together.
• Do give children separate rooms, if possible. Crowding children into small spaces doesn't promote harmony. A child's room should be a sacred place.
• When a fight breaks out, confine children to their rooms for thirty minutes without radio or TV. After that, give them different jobs to do.
• Do insist that children respect the possessions of others.
• Do insist that nothing is to be taken or borrowed from a sibling without permission.
• Do spend some one-on-one time with each child. This helps keep quarreling in check. Boys quarrel less when fathers spend time with them.
• Do remember that some boys don't need a reason to fight. They do it because it's fun for them.
• Do try to relax. Tense parents create a tense climate, which may produce tense kids. Tense kids pick fights.
• Do keep children busy when quarreling is a chronic problem. Idle children fight more frequently.
• Do be aware that certain combinations of children are combustible. A threesome may mean trouble.
• Do mediate quickly if quarreling starts.

If I were to sum up my thoughts in this chapter, I'd say, "Mom and Dad, hang in there. Time has a way of dulling swords. I know many children who fought like enemies as youngsters who are best of friends today. Then again, others still bicker, but they are more capable of putting on their best behavior in front of others. In either case, life gets more pleasant as they get older."

Thinking It Through

1. Some experts say that quarreling is to be expected and is sometimes useful. What do you think?

2. What do your children usually quarrel about?

3. As a mother, how do you usually respond to your children's quarrels?

4. What do you think about the idea of letting children settle their own battles?

5. Do you feel it is your job as a Christian mother to make your children love one another?

6. Do you expect your children to share their possessions with their siblings? Do they follow through, or does
this cause problems?

7. How do you protect yourself from showing favoritism
with your children?

8. Toward the end of the chapter, I listed some *do*s and
*don't*s for parents when their children fight. List two
things you will try to *do* the next time your kids fight.

9. List two things that you will *not do* the next time your
kids fight.

10. What have you learned from this chapter that you
can share with one other mother this week? When and
with whom will you do this?

9

Maturity Is Bred, Not Born ━━━━━━━━━━━ ▪▪

When my little ones were born, there were times I felt overwhelmed by the awesome responsibility of parenting. Lyall and I were the first significant people in their lives. We fashioned their environment and had tremendous opportunities to mold their personalities. Believe me, that was both marvelous and frightening at the same time.

We were like most couples. Even though we were deeply in love, we struggled to adjust to each other after walking down the aisle. When the babies came, we struggled to adjust to them. It was work. But I'm convinced that one of the greatest favors we did for our children was to make our marriage our first priority and them the second.

It's vitally important that husbands and wives go to great lengths to understand and care for each other. If they don't, they will undercut the security of their children. Children feel settled when parents love each other. They think, "Mom and Dad love each other. Even when they argue, they stay together. They aren't going to leave each other, or me." This kind of assurance helps them grow up confident, balanced, and assured.[1]

For the two-parent home, partnership is more important than parenthood, because the partnership often determines the quality of parenthood. It's not how you treat children as much as how you treat each other.

Sometimes parents miss this point. Years ago, I counseled a couple who had five children. Their situation was somewhat peculiar. Bob, the husband, told me he loved being a father. "I can't wait to get home after work to see my kids. They line up on the sofa and look out the window when I pull in the driveway. I feel like a king going to his castle. At work, I don't have a prestigious position, but I don't mind. I live for my kids."

Bob grew up in a large family where there was never quite enough of anything. They were usually short of money, clothes, and food, but they were a happy bunch. As a child he fantasized about his future family. "I saw myself at one end of the dining table, my wife at the other, and children lined up along both sides."

He continued, "I love to take my children shopping and to show them off when they are nicely dressed. But my wife is sloppy and won't help the children look neat." Then the expression on his face darkened, and in a sober voice he said, "I love my kids, but ma'am, my wife disgusts me."

Bob had made the mistake of putting his kids before his wife. As the gap grew between them, their quarreling became more intense. He hated her housekeeping, and she was hurt by his criticism. Eventually the marriage dissolved. Their children suffered tremendous emotional pain that affected every area of their lives.

Countless women make the same mistake. Their kids come first, and their husband gets the leftovers. I have actually heard women say they married primarily to have kids. As soon as the babies were born, 99.9 percent of their energy was channeled toward their children, rather than toward meeting their husbands' needs. These mothers go out for lovely dates with their husbands, but their minds are on the kids all night. Their dinner conversation is strictly about the children. They leave the table before dessert arrives to call the baby-sitter and check on the home front. An hour after the movie has started, they call again. Their husbands' best efforts cannot shake them loose from dwelling on their babes.

I sometimes wonder if mothers aren't mothers until the day they die. My own mother constantly worried about her children, even after they were married. One day my father told her, "Edith, you never stop worrying about the children. They can manage now. I cannot share your concerns with you. I intend to live a happy life, now that we are retired, and I cannot be bothered with worries."

Mother used to fret about Lyall and I having so little money as full-time Christian workers. She hated my shabby clothes and the fact that at that point we didn't own a home for raising our children. When I see her in the future, I will probably say, "Mum, it was good for me. It made a 'man out of me,' and I needed it."

The struggle is typical. It's difficult to balance the roles of parent and spouse. But let me encourage men and women: When your partner takes first priority, parenting will be much easier.

A little boy is keen at sensing Mom and Dad's "togetherness." When love and affection are demonstrated between them, he feels secure. When they are absent, he feels turmoil, and this can lead to emotional crippling. A court judge in Denver who has handled over 28,000 delinquency cases once said, "The lack of affection between father and mother is the greatest cause of delinquency I know."[2]

In some cases, couples adjust well to each other but not to their children. Perhaps they don't like being committed to more than one person. Maybe they thrive on the challenge of a chase and conquest and grow bored with a settled life.

There are restless people who simply do not enjoy a

binding commitment. They hate reporting in every night and being tied to a changeless routine. They typically rebel against responsible family life because it leaves them little liberty. When their focus shifts from the person they love to the bondage that came with the institution of marriage, they usually run, leaving broken lives behind them. This happens much too often.

I recently talked with Tom and Patsy about their struggles in adjusting to parenthood. Tom hated going home at night because his boys were rambunctious and loud. Patsy had cabin fever from being cooped up with these rascals around the clock. Both parents were quiet, gentle people, and the quarreling between their boys raised the hair on the back of their necks.

Tom told me, "I hate being with those kids. They get on my nerves. When I come home from work, I want to relax and have some time to myself. At work I'm under pressure all day long, and people constantly need my attention. When I get home, I need some 'nothing time' and my own quiet space with no intruders. If I have a few minutes to myself, then I think I'll be able to cope with the family better.

"But that isn't what happens. As soon as I walk in the door, Patsy starts unloading on me and the boys claw for my attention. I feel like I want to run away from it all. Lately I've been dropping into a tavern nearby, just to relax. I care a lot about Patsy, but I don't enjoy the responsibilities of a family."

Patsy had as many complaints as Tom, and I applauded this couple for talking openly about their feelings. This helped them adjust better to parenthood. As time passed, they made some changes to make their family life more enjoyable. Patsy arranged things so Tom could have one-half hour of "nothing time" when he got home from work, and Tom began taking the boys on regular outings so Patsy could have time alone, too. The boys' bedtime was moved back to 8:30 P.M. so the couple could spend quiet evenings together.

Tom and Patsy learned that marriage is a process of adjustment, and in order to enjoy each other and their children, they had to be willing to be flexible. There were instances when they both had to change. Sometimes only slight modifications were necessary, but other times more drastic steps were needed for them to find contentment.

I talked with another couple, Cindy and Duane, about similar struggles they were having adjusting to parenthood. Cindy never expected to have a bunch of boys. She is a very petite, feminine woman who grew up with three sisters. With three sons, her frustrations were intense.

"Before the boys were born, I used to think about the fun I would have taking care of baby girls. I guess I figured that if I had boys, my husband would take over and I'd more or less follow along.

"Things didn't turn out that way. Duane rarely spends time with the boys. He says he's too busy trying to support us. When he was small, he was the only child of a widow and was used to a quiet, orderly home. He can't seem to handle the boys if they are noisy or quarrel. Is there something wrong with Duane? Why doesn't he enjoy his own sons?"

I tried to explain to Cindy that often our dreams of an ideal family don't come true. It's been my observation during thirty years of counseling that there are many men like Duane who do not enjoy aspects of family life. Duane did not have a childhood that prepared him for three rowdy boys. Cindy was better equipped because she grew up with several other siblings and was accustomed to more noise, music, pranks, and laughter.

Duane was in a time of life when he needed to make three main adjustments. He had to adjust to providing for five people, to being a husband, and to being a father. He was accomplishing two of the three quite well, but the fathering role was still difficult for him. Cindy seemed to receive some consolation from knowing that not many men are balanced in all three areas all the time.

I want to make an important point here. Many of the difficulties that arise in parenting and marriage have workable solutions. If a couple is willing to communicate honestly, they can become well-adjusted parents and grow to love their family. If they don't understand why they are having problems, or what their problems are, they should get objective help from a counselor. Without information, conditions will not improve. Without improvement, friction will escalate, and children in the home may become emotionally insecure. This in turn will stifle their development toward maturity.

Building Emotional Maturity

What are some of the factors which, when set in a background of love for the child, help make a normal male personality? In the physical sense, the answer is fairly easy. We know about the importance of fresh air, sunshine, cleanliness, proper food, exercise, and protection from disease. Unfortunately we know far less about a boy's psychological needs. These are much less tangible.

If there were a formula for building an emotionally secure boy, India rubber might be the main ingredient, because a great deal of flexibility is needed. There are seven characteristics, however, that a child must have if he is to grow into an emotionally mature adult:[3]

- A desire to move
- A readiness and willingness to imitate
- An alert response to suggestion
- A reasonable love of power
- A strong level of curiosity
- A dash of childhood savagery
- A spark of romancing

These are the foundation stones of emotional maturity for boys. Let's look at each one in turn.

A Desire to Move

Mothers should encourage their babies to reach, crawl, and explore their environment. The mother who boasts that her little boy is always quiet and well behaved is not informed. A psychologically docile child is not a normal child.

A Willingness to Imitate

Language is learned primarily through imitation. The child hears sounds and sees behavior related to those sounds. Male and female roles are also learned through imitation. Children will try to replicate the character qualities they see in their parents. Honesty, truthfulness, courage, reflection, judgment, tolerance, patriotism—all are learned attitudes. People with these character qualities should be an active part of a boy's life, so he can copy them. He will mirror what he sees.

An Alert Response to Suggestion

Normal children respond to hundreds of suggestions and follow them when they come from authority figures like parents. Suggestion can be a useful psychological tool for shaping the personality of a child. There are, however, those humorous occasions when the power of suggestion doesn't work. A mother had a brother who was a famous bridge-building engineer. She said to her son, "I suppose you are going to be a great engineer like your uncle." Her son replied, "No, I think I'm going to be neurotic like my father." His father was always moaning about his aches and pains, especially during mealtime gatherings.

A Reasonable Love of Power

A love of power begins in childhood, and this element influences a boy's leadership capabilities. Notice the word *reasonable* in this phrase. It's important for parents to direct and control their son's love of power so it doesn't get out of hand. A father who is a courteous, patient, and kind authority figure at home can model an appropriate use of power for his son.

"Unwise, and questionably kind adults often permit children to hang onto their babyhood power over long. Sometimes this spoiling is pseudoscientifically camouflaged as 'letting the children express themselves.' "[4]

I remember an incident that happened with a little boy who had an *un*reasonable and unharnessed love of power. Rita and her son, Tom, came to stay with us while her husband was abroad for additional short-term schooling. Since Tom's father had a job that required many hours of his time, and he was rarely home, Rita and Tom were unusually close.

While they were in our home for four weeks, my children were shocked by Tom's behavior. Even though he was a small child he definitely ruled his mother. At meals Tom refused to eat many ordinary foods, including all vegetables. Every meal was a battle. Tom got his way, and his mother, in tears, pleaded with him to eat his meat and greens. "Tom, you know how important it is for you to eat. Your doctor says you are too thin. You must eat."

"You know I hate vegetables, and I'll never eat them," he replied.

Believe it or not, after every meal Rita gave Tom candy. She was afraid he would become weak without something in his stomach. The story sounds ridiculous, but it actually happened in my home. Rita was completely controlled by this boy.

After they had been with us a couple of weeks, Rita received an invitation to lead some women's Bible studies. This meant she had to leave Tom with us for an entire week. She was very undecided about leaving, but I encouraged her to go. Before she left, she bought a big bag of candy for me to give Tom if he went on a hunger strike. On the outside, I kept calm and cool, but on the inside, I was roaring with laughter. Little did she know what I had in mind for Tom while she was gone! Believe me, it wasn't candy.

The first meal we had together, I put a tiny serving of food on his plate and ignored him. It wasn't long before we heard the usual.

"Auntie Jean, I never eat carrots. They make me sick."

"Tom, everybody eats carrots in this house," I replied.

"My mother will think you're cruel to me."

"Your mother will be pleased that we fed you carrots, because she knows you need good food."

"If you make me eat this nasty food, I'll get sick and you'll have to call the doctor."

"Our doctor wouldn't come. He's too busy for that kind of problem."

Finally, David jumped into the conversation and retorted, "Boys have to eat to get bigger than girls. You're a sissy, not a boy!"

The battle dragged on, and I realized that once again Tom was the power figure. He had reigned supreme in his world ever since he was born. He had usurped the power of control from his weak, indulgent mother and absentee father.

Eventually I took a risk and said, "Tom, you will eat a tiny serving of everything we are eating, and you will stay at the table until you do." He turned white and squealed, "You wouldn't be that cruel to me!"

Tom looked at my determined face again and grabbed his fork. Shoveling food into his mouth as fast as his hands would work, he gulped the meat and vegetables down with water. Next he announced he was sick and it was all my fault.

By the end of the week, Tom was a different boy, and we had all grown to really like him. He was consuming large helpings of food and took pride in eating grated raw carrots like the others. He even boasted that he could eat more than my daughter Heather. He still begged for candy, but since it had been previously used as a reward for his defiance, I decided to hide the bag. No one ate candy that week.

Now here is the tragedy of the story. When Rita came home, Tom ran into her arms saying, "Auntie Jean made me eat all the things that make me sick, and I didn't feel well all week."

Without even questioning his tale, she said, "Oh, darling, I have missed you so much. I'll never leave you again. I brought some new chocolates home for you. I'll get them right away."

I couldn't believe what I saw. Tom knew exactly how to punish his mother for leaving him. I've never seen a child reign with such absolute power. The whole situation was pathetic.

A Strong Level of Curiosity

Parents do their son a favor by encouraging him to investigate. They can strengthen his level of curiosity by prompting his inquisitive mind and exposing him to problem-solving situations. I realize this requires time and patience from parents, but the results are worth it.

Were it not for the potential of curiosity in human beings, we would have none of the benefits of modern life. Wonder drugs like penicillin and streptomycin, and all the home convenience gadgets, were all born out of curiosity. "Science is applied curiosity. The true scientist takes things apart and puts them together, just like little boys love to do."[5]

Jenny Churchill was particularly skilled at developing Winston's curiosity. She didn't have answers to all his political questions, but she did introduce him to people who helped satisfy his inquisitive mind. I think it's amazing that she frequently took him to the House of Commons debates as a twelve-year-old.

Let me reiterate a point I mentioned earlier: Parents must not fear their child's sexual curiosity. It's absolutely normal and such a strong human trait that it's classified as an instinct. If a boy's sexual curiosity is forced into concealment, it redoubles its intensity. What's a parent to do? Be informed and truthfully answer your son's questions. Send away for information if the subject makes you uneasy.

A Dash of Savagery

When I use the term *savagery*, I don't mean a boy should be ruthless or cruel. Rather he must learn to strive and fight for himself, in order to survive in this world. When he's young, this skill can be developed within the context of competitive activities.

There is a tendency in some schools these days to abolish competition. If this is taken too far, little boys will be robbed of necessary character training. Adult life involves stiff competition. Little boys must be prepared for this and ready to experience the satisfaction of victory and the disappointment of defeat.

The average classroom can provide many opportunities for boys to learn how to strive. A bulletin board can be used to display outstanding work such as the funniest story, the most colorful painting, or the most original drawing in the class. Parents can encourage savagery by supporting their son's school projects. These opportunities give him a chance to compete, learn how to finish tasks, and aim at high standards of performance.

I realize not all little boys want to compete. There are those who are content to do passing work and nothing more. They feel they can never beat the talented or brainy kids, so they develop an attitude of mediocrity and are satisfied to slide through life. These are the children that teachers and parents have to push, encourage, reward, and provide with creative avenues of competition.

When I was a teenager, I entered a very prestigious private girls' school that was famous for its achieving scholars. It was a discouraging experience, because I felt I couldn't compete with the other girls. They were far more intelligent, and their scholastic brilliance was known all over the world. I begged my parents to let me drop out and return to my former school, but they were adamant that I complete the school year before I made a change.

Sports were very important at the school, and the girls on the A teams were heroines. My parents saw this and provided tennis coaching for me, along with some costly new spiked running shoes. They even let me out of home responsibilities so I could have more time to practice. I cannot exaggerate the impact my success in tennis had on my development that year. I never thought I would make it at that school, but after I found my niche, I realized I could stand tall with the best of them. With my parents' support, I learned how to strive, which enabled me to survive.

Dr. Harvey Kaufman, a prominent psychiatrist, said, "A grown man finds his adult male maturity in the arena of his vocation."[6] Notice how Dr. Kaufman carefully chose the word *arena*. It evokes thoughts of an open sandy place where gladiators fought spirited battles in Roman amphitheaters.

In today's society we don't fight with swords and shields. But a man is called upon to enter into contest every day at work. Even in very simple jobs, he must compete in order to hold his position. On more advanced levels, he must strive to prove he is the victor, for other trained gladiators with sharpened swords want his job.

Living as a Christian in this world is warfare. The Scriptures are filled with fighting, resisting, and conquering. Aggressiveness in faith and resistance to evil are commanded by the Lord. Old Testament books speak of numerous contests fought in direct obedience to God.

It isn't unspiritual to nurture savagery in little boys. It's a necessity. If they are to survive in this world, they must learn how to strive in their areas of interest and in their personal walk with God. Then they can look back over their lives like Paul and say, "I have fought a good fight,

I have finished my course, I have kept the faith" (2 Timothy 4:7 KJV).

A Spark of Romancing

When I use the word *romancing*, I am referring to the budding of a boy's imagination. Little boys need to develop the ability to dream, envision, and fantasize. This is a topic that must be handled delicately, because there are many games on the market today that misuse and overindulge children's imagination. Fantasy games or TV shows that promote negative imagination and role playing can actually damage a child's normal development.

Balance is needed. Many boys feel blocked from expressing their creativity. There is a taboo in our society about boys being tender, sensitive, and creative. In many circles the boy who is interested in art, music, or writing automatically declines in value as a male. Psychiatrists are concerned because the American masculine ideal seems to equate virility with physical strength and athletic prowess. The ideal of a healthy male who is both strong and tender is being replaced by the image of an aggressive superman whose arrogant self-centeredness is glorified.

Parents must not forget that some boys are more intellectually and musically gifted than physically strong. Their talents need to be nurtured, even if they don't fit into the stereotypical, pseudomasculine ideal that prevails in today's society.

As a little boy, my husband, Lyall, had many artistic and creative talents. He was raised on a sheep station that his ancestors established in south Australia. Many of the others in his family carried on the work one generation after another. His brothers actually furthered the development of a new breed of sheep. But Lyall was different. His first love was art. From the time he was three, he enjoyed drawing pictures. As a boy he made contacts with leading illustrators and cartoonists and received lessons from them.

No one in Lyall's family had similar interests. They were more rugged and enjoyed hard physical work. But they never laughed at Lyall or made him feel inferior. The only negative memory Lyall recalls was a comment his father made. "My boy—we eat sheep. But you cannot eat your art!" (The culture his father was raised in had one message—a real man conquers the land and doesn't abandon his heritage.) For the most part, though, Lyall's family was fascinated by his abilities and encouraged him to pursue his dream of becoming a portrait painter. They nurtured the spark of romancing in him, and in time, his dream came true.

What Is Your Son's Maturity Quotient?

We have reviewed seven characteristics parents can nurture to help their sons toward maturity. But what is maturity? How will you know if your son has reached this goal? We must begin by defining maturity, and we will do this by listing ten characteristics of a mature male. To find your son's maturity quotient, simply place a check in the left-hand column if you can agree with the statement.[7]

My son . . .
____ has the ability to stick to a job
____ has the capacity to give more to a job than is requested
____ is reliable
____ is persistent to carry out a plan regardless of difficulties
____ has the ability to work with other people under organization and authority
____ has the ability to make decisions
____ has a will to live
____ is flexible
____ has established independence
____ is tolerant of others

Total the statements with which you agreed. If you marked 7–10, your son is well on the way to maturity. If you marked 5–7, your son has made progress, but has some work ahead. If you marked 0–4, you and your son have your work cut out for you!

Thinking It Through

1. What do you think about the idea that partnership is more important than parenting?

2. Which was more challenging for you, adjusting to marriage or adjusting to parenthood? Please explain.

3. Dr. Douglas Anderson said, "Marriage is a place of soul growth." What does that mean to you?

4. What are some ways a mother can balance her relationships with her husband and their children?

5. How are you nurturing "savagery" and a "spark of romancing" in your children?

6. Do you think that competition should be modified in our Western culture?

7. If Tom's mother came to you for advice about raising her son, what would you say to her?

8. How do you encourage your children to think? Give an example.

9. What is one thing you learned from this chapter that you can share with another person? When and with whom will you do this?

10

Hormonal Phases of a Mother's Life ⬛

Statistics show that most mothers are in their midthirties to early forties when their sons reach puberty. This is a challenging time for mother-son relationships due to hormonal changes happening in *both* their bodies. We have discussed these changes in boys. This book would be incomplete without addressing the hormone fluctuations that occur in women during these years. It is important for mothers to understand that their emotional responses may be strongly influenced by their bodies. A bit of knowledge in this area can help settle a frazzled woman who feels like resigning from motherhood!

Personality and Hormones

In 1983 Niels H. Lauersen, M.D., and Eileen Stukane wrote a book titled *Premenstrual Syndrome and You.* These words appeared on the cover:

"Over 5 million women are in the dark about a severe hormonal imbalance affecting them 10 days out of every month. They are frightened by violent fluctuations in mood, depression, and weight gain, and they don't know what's causing them."

With all the information that has been distributed over the last few years through books, magazines, and television, I thought women could easily find answers about how monthly hormone changes affect their physical, psychological, social, and emotional life. The truth is that many women aren't familiar with this information and have been told their problems are in their heads. This is poppycock! There is clear evidence that a woman's menstrual cycle can drastically affect the way she feels about herself, her husband, her children, her profession, her ministry, and so forth. You name it; it's affected.

Most women will have a monthly menstrual cycle for forty years of their lives. During each month, two ovarian hormones have great impact on a woman's emotions. Estrogen dominates the preovulation phase, and progesterone affects the postovulation phase.

Many women may have five changes in their personality within each menstrual cycle. Though the actual symptoms a woman experiences may vary from month to month, the monthly phases tend to be cyclic. I'd like to draw an analogy between these phases and the seasons of the year.

Phase 1: The Spring Phase

This phase starts with the blood flow of the menstrual cycle and is dominated by estrogen. During this time, a woman feels bright and fresh, like spring. New surges of life burst inside her. She is positive, assertive, outgoing, happy, energetic, and well coordinated. Little threatens her, and she feels she can accomplish almost anything. Her relationship with her husband and kids is delightful and relaxed. The tension she felt prior to her period vanishes, and life is a whole new ball game.

Phase 2: The Summer Phase

This is a peaceful, happy, affirming, creative time of the month. A woman has "warm fuzzies" for her family and friends and is generally pleased with life. She is a bit less assertive than in the spring phase, but able to accomplish much. Her body is moving toward liberating an egg for fertilization. Estrogen continues to dominate.

Phase 3: The Midsummer Phase

Midsummer is that short time during which ovulation occurs. The egg leaves the ovary for possible fertilization. A woman usually feels euphoric, motherly, peaceful, sensual, and integrative. Everything in life seems absolutely wonderful. She loves her husband and kids, who can do no wrong. All of these feelings are influenced by progesterone production.

Phase 4: The Fall Phase

Immediately after ovulation, a woman begins to slowly lose energy as she enters the fall phase. Slight depression or the doldrums set in, and she isn't as enthusiastic about life as she was a few days ago. Suddenly her husband and children don't seem quite so lovable. Assertiveness is a thing of the past, and her confidence is droopy. It is generally suspected that during the fall and winter phases, hormone fluctuations are responsible for a host of unpleasant symptoms.

Phase 5: The Winter Phase

Winter sets in around the fourth week of the menstrual month, and many women become downright witchy. There are typical symptoms associated with this phase:

Unspiritual feelings	Sudden mood swings
No concentration	Temper outbursts
Lowered reaction time	Uptight, can't relax
Sluggish	Jittery and tremors
Needs extra sleep	Loss of self-control
Depressed, tired	Loss of security
Nervous tension	Frustration
Irritable	Agitation
Savage	Fears of losing control
Weepy	Restless energy

Outbursts of emotion
Jumpiness
High-strung temperament
Abnormal excitement
Manic activity
Hair-trigger temperament
Recurrent frenzy or catatonic depression
Hypermanic trends
Impaired self-control
Impaired judgment
Impaired willpower
Hazy thinking
Change in sexual behavior
Spending sprees
Striking change of behavior
Spectacular alteration of behavior
Foreboding sensation of impending insecurity
Cyclic alteration of personality
Expressed resentment
Expressed hostility
Rattled
Captious
Hypercritical
Biting in speech
Lashes out for no reason
Suspicious
Jealous
Distrustful
Low self-esteem
Apprehension
Anxiety
Forgetfulness
Fretfulness
Lethargic
Sluggish
Moody and mood swings
Crying over anything
Talking too much or not at all
Feeling of fatigue
Blanket-of-fog feeling
Sense of loss
Desire to be alone
Melancholia
Careless
Thoughtless
Unpunctual
Absent-minded
Morbid memories
Supersensitive
Horrid
Irrational
Hateful
Shouts
Fights
No insights
Mistakes—accidents
Impulsive
Split-personality feeling
Self-depreciation
Negative attitudes to self
Negative attitudes to others
Abnormally hungry
Food binges
Masculine foods wanted
Salty foods
Tolerance for sugar
Cravings for foods
Compulsive eating
Touch-me-not
Irritated whenever hungry

Fortunately, the menstrual flow is only a few days away, and a woman will feel quite different once this begins. However, some women suffer somatic symptoms like stomach cramps, backaches, or headaches after their periods start.

During the winter phase, a wife may feel very negative about her husband and say things like, "I wish I never married you in the first place. I hate my life. I might have had a great career if I had not married you." Her son might see her throw a temper tantrum simply because he left his bike in the middle of the driveway or his socks on the floor.

What are these poor males supposed to think when they face these tirades? Why is their wife and mother acting this way? Two weeks before, she was warm, charming, and making their favorite meals. Now she is crabby, feeding her face with junk food, and harping at them for every little thing they do. Who is this lady?

May I make a suggestion? Women, do yourself a favor. Inform your husbands and older sons about these five phases so they know what to expect. They are likely to think you're going crazy once a month, year after year, if they don't understand what's happening in your body. It will be much easier for them to tolerate your mood swings if they are informed.

The Slump

During my clinical practice, I noticed that women in their late thirties and early forties reported major changes in their attitudes, feelings, and health. It seemed I kept hearing the same story over and over again from scores of women. I didn't understand everything I heard, but I did believe them.

I could not imagine why energetic and very functional women were suddenly feeling lethargic and hopeless. Many were frightened about these changes and felt over-

whelmed by ordinary duties they had successfully handled for years. Apparently nothing was physically wrong,
but they felt they had to drag themselves through each
day, just to keep going. Some wondered if they were
beginning early menopause, but medical doctors said no,
then handed the women antidepressants and told them to
see a counselor or psychiatrist.

Now we understand more about the emotional phases
of a woman's life. Typical symptoms associated with
hormonal changes during the late thirties and early forties
are:

- Drop in energy level that seems a nuisance
- A dragging feeling on some days
- A listless feeling on some days
- Loss of interest or need for sex—some say it's boring
- Earlier interests don't seem important anymore
- Boredom with duties
- Mild depression unrelated to menstrual cycle
- The blahs
- Foreboding feelings on some days
- Feelings of morbidness or sadness on some days
- Overreaction to small irritations
- Touchiness
- Weepiness
- Feelings of craziness ("I'm bursting apart at the
  seams.")
- Difficulty in making small or large decisions
- Memory lapses
- Feelings of failure
- Feeling unneeded or useless
- Spiritual worries ("I wonder if I'm really a Christian.")
- Fantasies about a true love yet to emerge
- Interest in romantic novels and love stories
- Compulsive buying
- Increase of daydreaming—fantasies of escape from the
  present

- Recapitulation feelings ("If only I could live my life over again.")
- Regrets over past decisions or choices
- Worry over past mistakes
- Increased introspection
- Concerns about early menopause

Not long ago, I took this list of symptoms and surveyed over seventy-five women in the Northwest. The five symptoms that most frequently bothered these women were: (1) a sudden drop in energy, (2) unusual irritability, (3) touchiness/overreacting, (4) mild depression, and (5) loss of interest in highly valued activities.

It Wasn't in Her Head

Many years ago a forty-one-year-old husband sought counsel from me concerning his wife's health. He had six lovely children and told me his wife was a wonderful person. But he was worried.

"I work two jobs in order to feed eight of us. We both agree Margaret shouldn't work while the children are growing up. Even though my hours are long, I'm basically content with my lot in life. Margaret seemed to feel the same way, until recently."

"Do you mean she had a sudden change of attitude?" I inquired.

"That's hard to answer," he replied. "I feel like saying yes *and* no to your question."

I probed further. "Can you remember an event or crisis that preceded her changes?"

"I guess I first noticed she was acting different last summer at a family reunion. This is a great affair that Margaret looks forward to every year. It's the only time all her family is together in one large group.

"Last summer she seemed happy about the upcoming reunion and cooked three days straight to prepare for the event. But, Mrs. Lush, the strangest thing happened at that party. When we were all together at lunch, she suddenly flew into a rage over something she was discussing with her favorite sister. Her tirade went on and on. I was stunned, because I had never seen her act that way. The incident ruined the party for Margaret, and she felt totally humiliated by her overreaction. She and her sister later talked and worked things out between themselves.

"That was nearly a year ago. Since then she has seemed rather listless, with little energy or interest in things around her. She cries a lot and says nobody needs her. But, Mrs. Lush, that isn't true. She's the center of our family, and we all love her very much.

"Margaret used to be a garage-sale and flea-market buff. She made beautiful crafts and enjoyed being creative in the kitchen. Now she doesn't seem to care about doing anything. Please, Mrs. Lush, tell me how I can help her."

I have never forgotten this honest plea for help. A week later I met with Margaret, and her story duplicated her husband's. I wondered if the picnic incident was causing her present low spirits, but concluded that it wasn't that simple. There was more to the picture than I could see. I was stumped. Something was happening that I didn't understand.

After this case, I watched and listened to women in their late thirties and early forties in a new way. After many years of clinical investigation, I started to broadcast my findings with Dr. James Dobson. His radio program, "Focus on the Family," was flooded with responses from the listening audience, and the phone calls and letters continue to come five years later.

One woman called from the East Coast after hearing the broadcast. Extremely upset, she said, "I have just heard your broadcast, and your descriptions fit me. There are times when life seems unbearable. I feel like I have crazy days. Some mornings I wake up and feel like I'm losing my mind!"

When she said she was forty-three, I thought, *That figures*. I told her I had heard this from numerous other women in their early forties, and I tried to offer encouragement.

"I know what you are experiencing, and you are not going crazy. Your body is going through some changes and influencing your mind to make you think you are going crazy. I know the scary feelings you have are very real, and not looney fantasies. These panic attacks may be closely associated with hormonal fluctuations that occur in women during their late thirties and early forties."

"Oh!" she exclaimed. "You mean my body is sending these crazy ideas to my mind, and my mind isn't really crazy after all?"

"Yes, that's right," I replied.

"Well, that's the best news I've heard in months. I can live with that much easier than thinking I'm going out of my mind!"

I assured her that if that were the case, hundreds of other women who called me were going crazy, too. For further information, see my book, *Emotional Phases of a Woman's Life*. This book explores the various phases of a woman's life, examining the hormonal changes that at times seem to govern her body and mind. As each phase is discussed, hope and help is offered to those who feel victimized by their hormones.

Thinking It Through

1. Do you notice changes in your moods and body during certain times each month? Explain.

2. How does this affect your role as a wife?

3. What do you do to help yourself cope with the challenges of the winter phase?

4. We mentioned "the slump" that many women experience in their late thirties and early forties. Have you or anyone else you know experienced this?

5. How have hormone fluctuations affected the way you relate to your children?

6. Most men say, "I'll never be able to understand women!" What can you do to help your husband better understand your emotional life?

7. Do you think it would be appropriate to discuss the information in this chapter with a teenage son?

8. What is one new idea you learned in this chapter?

9. What have you learned from this chapter that you can share with a friend? When and with whom will you share this information?

11

What About Single Moms? ▦

During my thirty years of counseling, there have been two types of mothers for whom I have carried a tremendous burden: the single mother and the stepmother. Both have been forced to make traumatic transitions.

Becoming a single mother involves more than losing a husband. It may also mean a drop in income, a loss of family friends, and the loss of a home. All of a sudden the chief cook and bottle washer also has to be the gardener, repairman, and auto mechanic.

The abruptness with which some women are thrown into this role can make life seem utterly unbearable. I have wept with these women. I have agonized with them over their losses. I have felt their fear as they faced a competitive job market without any training. Frankly, I would like to close my eyes to these kinds of problems because of the heartache they bring me. But that would not be fair. These women need help. They need love. They need someone's time.

Married, Now Single

Six years ago I looked like a typical pastor's wife. My life revolved around my husband and kids. I was married, had two darling children, and was part of a wonderful congregation. Our home was lovely, friends were plentiful, and I was enjoying an exciting re-entry into the teaching profession.

Our marriage wasn't perfect. Communication was undermined by fatigue and nonstop routines. Church crises, building programs, meetings, school activities, and two growing children ate away at our relationship.

One Sunday morning my husband preached his sermon and took the children out for doughnuts. The next day he was gone. I later found out he was in love with another woman.

After the shock wore off, grief began. Waves of anger, guilt, fear, and self-reproach kept washing over me. I cried all the time and found it impossible to smile. It took all my energy to do my job, cook, run the kids to their activities, clean, and go to sleep in an empty bed. Feelings of rejection and failure were like crystals of salt rubbed into my open wounds.

I had lost my mate, half of my whole. I am now a divorcée. My children lost their father. Jenny used to cry because she missed "Daddy's kisses." Now, as a twelve-year-old, she keeps her life private and is very independent.

Allen was ten when his father left. He is now fifteen and worries he won't be able to handle relationships with girls. For three years after his father told him good-bye, he slipped into my room at night to sleep on the floor by my bed. He didn't let me hug or kiss him for fear he would become a "mama's boy." Those were his words.

Just this year Allen finally found the courage to express his anger at his father and me. He resents other boys with fathers who do things with them. He feels ashamed and different from other kids. When he went on a high school church retreat, the speaker said the kids needed to know their earthly father in order to understand their heavenly Father. Can you imagine his confusion? He came home convinced he couldn't know God like other kids because his father wasn't around anymore.

I hated Sundays, even though I loved Jesus with all my heart. Sundays brought church, and church is built around families. It takes a long time to accept the idea that one mother and two children still constitute a family. People may love you, but they don't entertain you for long. When I visited churches with my kids, we were sometimes greeted and sometimes ignored.

I remember feeling like such a failure at times—so weak and unable to handle the divorce, the kids, and the financial pressures. In one of my toughest moments I called you, Jean. I'll never forget something you said to me: "There will be days that you are a success simply because you survived twenty-four hours." And then you said, "You must not expect yourself to function in five-speed overdrive. Shift down to survival gear." I clung to that every night while I was trying to fall asleep.

Today I can say I have survived. There are even days I feel happy and in control of my situation. But I have to be on guard against self-pity, especially when I'm weary and just before payday. Working has saved my sanity. For eight hours each day it forced me to be appropriate. It filled my days with people, many of whom cared for me in tangible ways.

My children have grieved and have learned that we are still a family. Their courage, honesty, and resilience have awed me. Their capacity to love me when I had so little to give was incredible. They are more independent and have learned to think for themselves. They have had to struggle with the contradictions in Christian living and theology they see in their parents' life. At tender ages they have learned that faith in God sometimes means hanging in there when answers don't fit and prayers don't seem to be answered. Those are good lessons.

Jean, I can't imagine going through the past five years without your support. But most important of all, I can't imagine life without God. There have been many times when I didn't feel His presence, but I'm certain He was there. He is seeing us through these hardships and is very patient with our progress. His Word says He has special love for widows and children. I ask Him to love my kids the way they need to be loved. With His help, we will keep hanging in there, and we will survive.

I've lost count of the number of single mothers like Lorraine I've counseled over the years. Based on my experience, I am going to risk making a categorical statement: The Christian women who became single mothers grew to love God in ways they had never experienced during their married years. Their poverty, despair, and loneliness drove them to the heart of God, where they were touched by His grace. Years later many came back to see me, boasting of God's ability to carry them through their painful transition. Lorraine was one of those women.

Who Is My Dad?

Experts agree that children want both a mother and father. A child who lacks one or the other will often ask the remaining parent for a replacement. If necessary, he will create a replacement.

Years ago a worried mother consulted with me about her eight-year-old son, Bill. Apparently Bill could hardly read and was doing poorly in most of his subjects at school.

Tanya is different from all the other mothers mentioned in this book. She had been a prostitute for many years and didn't know who fathered her children. Nevertheless, Tanya was a dedicated mother who centered her life around her children. Bill was eight, and Susan was two. One afternoon Bill and his mother talked about his school-work.

"Bill, your teacher says you are an intelligent, bright boy, but that you are having trouble reading. Can you tell me what's wrong?" Tanya asked.

Catching her completely off guard, he said, "I will never learn to read until I can see my father's face. I'm not a real boy like all the other guys, because I don't have a father. The other kids say I'm weird because I tell them I never had a father. How could I be born without a father?"

Tanya was uncomfortable with the conversation, but after a pause and a deep breath, she finally said, "You do have a father somewhere."

Filled with glee, Bill said, "I do? Where's his picture? Show me. I want to see his face right now. Why didn't you tell me I had a dad? Quick? Go get his picture."

At this point, Tanya didn't know what to say, so she decided not to do anything until we had talked. When we met together, I realized Tanya had blocked memories of her prostitute relations and really didn't know who was Bill's actual father. She was hoping Bill would accept her as his only parent and believed that if she was a great parent, Bill would not need to know the ugly facts of her early life.

I explained it was imperative for her to search her memories for the facts. Deep down I suspected she had some idea of who may have fathered Bill. The thoughts had been suppressed for years, but somehow she needed to get in touch with them. She came in the following week and said she had narrowed down the possibilities to two men who could be Bill's father.

Eventually Tanya said she thought William, the musi-cian, was Bill's father. Not expecting a positive answer, I asked her if she had a picture of him. She wasn't certain, but said she would look through some old papers in a chest when she got home. I couldn't believe my eyes when she came in the following week. She had found a newspaper clipping that showed the band performing on an opening night. William's picture was front and center.

Now we had another problem to discuss. William was an alcoholic. What kind of role model would he be for Bill? The question was important, but more than anything else, Bill needed to know that he did have a father.

When Tanya showed Bill the picture of William, he was ecstatic. He wanted to know every detail about his newly discovered father. Her explanation was outstanding.

"Bill, you have a Dad, and as far as I know, he still lives in California. He's a musician and earns a living playing in a band. When I knew him, William had many problems. He drank all the time and could not stop himself. When I found out I was pregnant, I never told him. Instead I moved from California to Seattle to make a home for us before you were born. I was very young and had a lot of problems, too. I wanted to make a fresh start for you."

Bill wasn't concerned with the explanations; he was too impatient to listen any longer. He blurted out, "Well, why don't we go find William and tell him he has a son?"

Tanya called some bars where William regularly played and asked if he was still in the area. Believe it or not, she secured William's address, wrote him about Bill, and received a reply. William was going to travel to Alaska during the summer and said he would stop in Seattle on his way north.

I later learned that Bill met William. He never noticed that William was emaciated and reeked of alcohol. The thrill of meeting his father blinded him to those shortcomings. He was finally able to settle an issue that had haunted him for years. He no longer had to wonder, "Who is my dad?" After that encounter there was a marked improvement in Bill's schoolwork. His grades shot up, and his reading skills advanced each month. Tanya's courageous risk paid off.

Make Dad Look Good

Little boys don't simply have a desire for tokens of love from a father. They need to believe they are loved to develop a healthy personality. If they're convinced their father doesn't love them, they will feel resentful, turn their anger inward, and belittle themselves.[1]

I've worked with many depressed little boys who obsessively wanted love from fathers who had nothing to give them. Some of the fathers were completely absent, others were sporadically present. This put great pressure on Mom to create a good image of Dad. I know this is especially tough for a woman in a troubled marriage or a single mother who feels nothing but scorn for her ex-husband, but she must put her love for her child above her resentment and go out of her way not to paint a bad picture of Daddy.[2]

Betsy found it hard to say anything nice about her husband to anyone, including her kids. She had worked eight long years to put him through medical school and had two of his children. About a year after he set up his private practice, he dumped her and his two children for a younger nurse at the hospital. Now Betsy is alone, the sole support of the family.

I could understand why Betsy wanted full possession of her children after Pete's betrayal. Every summer I saw the anguish she experienced from sending the boys to visit their father. He was an expert at playing Santa Claus to win their approval and admiration, and he undermined her disciplinary actions.

On Sundays Pete fought to take the boys on special outings, arguing they shouldn't be forced to go to Sunday school. You can imagine the confusion this caused in those little boys. It was hard for Betsy not to strike back by tearing Pete down in front of the boys, but she knew the battle wasn't her children's. It was between two angry adults. Putting her kids in the middle of the tug-of-war wouldn't have been fair.

One of the hardest transitions Betsy had to make as a single mother was becoming the "bad guy" parent. Her husband used to share the discipline, but he became Mr. Nice Guy on the weekends, leaving her to be the one who had to keep the kids in check. That's a tough part to play, especially when she was already overloaded with her job and housework. But she dared not try to win her kids' love by being easy on them. They needed her consistent discipline even more than children in two-parent homes. And they had to hear her speak nicely about their father, or they would be the ones to suffer identity confusion.

Avoid Emotional Overload

"Mom, why didn't you get the chocolate cookies? I don't see them in the grocery bags," Adrian yelled, rummaging through the items on the counter.

"I already told you, Adrian. Our budget will not permit any extras this month," his mother, Pat, replied.

"Cookies aren't an extra! They are the only decent thing in my lunch."

"Adrian, I'm sorry. I couldn't stretch the budget to buy them this month."

"You're mean! You could have left off something else from the list. I bet the girls got what they wanted!" Adrian stormed out of the kitchen.

Adrian was an overweight eleven-year-old with a sister who was slightly older and a younger brother and sister. Pat had been home alone with the children since they were very small. Their sole support was her welfare check. She seemed to manage making ends meet and impressed me as a very bright and caring mother.

Although Adrian was a poor student, he never caused trouble at school. But his truculent attitude at home was growing worse by the day. Adrian constantly gave orders to his mother. Pat pleaded for him to understand her position and begged him to be nice. They had an odd mother-son relationship. Pat treated Adrian as a confidant rather than a son and detailed her problems to him.

I see this happen much too often, and children suffer in this kind of situation. I remember asking some children to tell me some of their secret wishes. One little eight-year-old girl said, "I wish more than anything else that my mom could have enough money to always pay bills on time." She was carrying a burden that was much too heavy for her.

Adrian carried a similar burden, and this made it difficult for Pat to discipline him. In a sense, Adrian controlled his mother, because Pat hated showdowns and took extreme measures to keep him happy.

About a year after I began working with this family, Pat became engaged to an old friend who had been very good to the entire family. The other children were happy about their new father-to-be, but Adrian was livid. You won't believe what he said to me.

"Mom is not going to do this *to me*. I never gave her permission, and I won't allow it!"

Surprised, I said, "What do you mean? Haven't you known about their relationship for a long time?"

"She never asked me if she could do this, and I refuse to let it happen," he retorted.

I explained to Adrian that he was going to have to accept his mother's decision. In a rage, he yelled, "I won't have it, and I will stop her!"

After the wedding, Adrian made life so unpleasant for the family that I suggested he stay with close relatives until he adjusted to the change.

Adrian had assumed the husband's role in the house, giving orders and taking charge as if he had the right to do so. I've seen this happen in many single-parent homes when a father is absent. It also happens in homes where a father is passive or overly absorbed in his own affairs. One child becomes a surrogate spouse and parent. The child who takes this role isn't necessarily a boy; it's whichever child the mother leans on and makes her close companion. This child helps meet his mother's emotional needs and shares the job of raising the other children. The problem is that children playing this role become overly responsible, and Moms lose authority and control.

Pat paid a high price for this surrogate relationship because Adrian demanded his wages any time he pleased. He knew there was an unwritten contract between himself and his mother. He met her needs in return for privileges and liberty. As in most cases like this, Adrian was unable to handle the power he gained.

This is a tough role for a child to play, because he is continually fed mixed messages. His mother unpredictably switches back and forth from wife to Mom. One moment she pours out her heart to him about the financial pressures she is under, and in the next breath she demands his obedience in straightening his room. The child becomes confused about which role is appropriate for him and doesn't know how to behave. This is what happened to Adrian. His childhood needs were never met because he was unable to accept necessary parental control. One of the reasons Adrian developed into an incorrigible human being was that he didn't have any consistent structures, rules, and limits throughout his early years.

It is usually very difficult for "surrogate husband" children like Adrian to accept their mother's marriage to another man. Some sons are forthright in their objections, but others don't openly show their anger. They silently sabotage. One little boy confided to me, "I hate him. He is so clean, he's neurotic. You just watch me get rid of him. My mom doesn't know what she's doing. I've got to protect her from that creep."

The new husband soon found trouble in his home. Feeling displaced by a rival, the boy treated his stepfather as an archenemy and made it clear there wasn't room for two husbands in one house.

What can a mother do to prevent this from happening in

her home? First, she must not view children as intimate friends. They cannot possibly meet her emotional needs. She needs adult companionship. She must also prevent herself from confiding details of personal issues to her children. The burden is too much for them to bear. I've seen too many little boys with ulcers who knew too much about their mothers' problems.

Mothers can protect their children from emotional over-load by building a support system with women who have similar challenges. Friendships with others are not a luxury, they are a necessity. Mothers can also prevent one child from becoming a surrogate parent by discreetly sharing their concerns with the entire family, rather than with a single child. This allows the family to face problems as a team and guards more mature children, who might assume the emotional support of the mother, from being elevated above others.

I also think it's crucial for children to know how to respond to parents who set them up as middlemen. Often I hear divorced parents tell their children things such as: "Tell your mother I don't like the way she uses your clothes money." Or, "Tell your father how mad I get when he calls after ten." Children who are put in this position can easily be taught to say, "If you don't like the way my mother (or father) does something, please talk to her (or him) about it, not me. I don't want to be in the middle of your disagreements."

What Can the Church Do?

All across America, more than 10 million single mothers face the challenge of raising their children alone. Figures from the census bureau show that nearly a quarter of all American children now live with one parent. In 89 percent of these single homes, mothers are the custodial parent. More than half of our country's children will spend some time in a single-parent household before they are eighteen years old.[3] Is it any wonder college students are watching reruns of "Ozzie and Harriet" and "Leave It to Beaver" to experience the nostalgia of an ideal family? Their own models don't exist anymore.

In light of these startling statistics, the church must become a place where these weakened families can receive strength and help. Sometimes the church is too concerned about its own growth, not about community effectiveness. I have seen this attitude much too often.

I remember a conversation I had with a church elder about the plight of single mothers. After I brought up the subject, I received a classic hackneyed answer that I have heard from several other church leaders, too.

I said to the elder of a large church, "I am concerned about the social problem in this nation. Millions of little boys are growing up without fathers at home, and I think their challenges are more serious than their sisters' because they may not have a close male model during their important developmental years. I cannot understand why churches are not doing much to meet this need. I see many outreach programs, but I rarely hear of an organized effort to reach fatherless boys."

"Oh, yes. I understand what you are saying," he replied. "I know there is a need in every church to do something more about this problem." His words were carefully chosen, and his tone of voice implied, "But don't bug us, lady." I pressed a bit more.

"Why can't several elders be assigned to help care for these needy families?"

"The issue has been raised before, and it's sticky. Most of the wives don't want their husbands to take on this kind of ministry. They are afraid the single mothers will become dependent and call their husbands whenever trouble arises."

It seems to me this is a lame excuse for doing nothing. Single mothers should be able to find a family within the church—the family of God. Their sons shouldn't have to depend entirely on secular boys' clubs to find a sense of belonging.

Fortunately some churches are beginning to respond. The single-parent ministry of First Evangelical Free Church in Fullerton, California, has hired the country's only full-time pastor to single parents. He directs a ministry that includes divorce recovery, day-care, financial aid, counseling, children's programs, camps and retreats, and missions trips to Mexico.[4]

University Presbyterian Church in Seattle began the Single Family Resource Network. The program operates on a simple foundation: Need is matched with the ability to alleviate that need. Lawyers take troublesome cases to court. Dentists fill teeth. Grandmas bake chocolate cookies and take children to the park.[5]

Easthill Church in Gresham, Oregon, offers Care Groups for single and two-parent families. Although the church has specific programs for singles, Pastor Ted Roberts feels Care Groups more effectively meet the needs of single-parent families. In place of an evening church service, forty groups meet two Sunday nights a month for fellowship. The home fellowships provide godly role models for children growing up in single-parent homes and offer support to mothers who are raising their children alone. Recreational outings are planned by each Care Group once a month. Boys without fathers at home have a chance to spend the day with other Dads and sons.

One couple from Aurora First Assembly in Granby, Colorado, arranged with a local supermarket to pick up all unsold bread and bakery items each Friday morning. Single mothers were then invited to swing by their home for their allotments.[6]

I've heard mixed reactions from single mothers about the help they find at church. Some say it's the most depressing place they know. Others receive comfort. Many of them know what kind of help they need but are afraid to ask. So I am going to ask for them. After a simple poll of single mothers, these are the things they most often requested:

- Offer divorce-recovery seminars. Single moms need support groups, not dating clubs.
- Provide a resource list that includes people from the church body who can help with fix-it jobs around the house for minimal fees. This will help avoid costly errors.
- Offer scholarships enabling children of single-parent families to attend youth events and retreats.
- If the church has a Christian school, offer scholarships for single-parent children.
- Organize the college group to offer free baby-sitting one weekend a month, so single moms can have a night out without the extra expense.
- Organize Sunday school classes to plan workdays a few times a year to help single mothers maintain their homes and yards.
- Start a grandparent adoption program. Children can look forward to a special outing with their "grandparents" once a month.
- Provide a chance for single parents to testify during church services about how God is helping them in the church body. This will sensitize others to the needs of these families.
- Make youth ministries a priority, so children from broken homes will discover that church can be fun. Youth activities will give them another chance to be around older godly men and women.
- Teach hospitality from the pulpit. Single-parent families need invitations for dinner, dessert, or even popcorn. Being in the home of a loving family can refresh a weary mom and work wonders for her children.

I cannot overemphasize the need for churches to teach hospitality. One single parent said, "When my son was severely injured two years ago, I was overwhelmed by the outpouring of support. A pastor visited almost every day. People sent flowers and cards. Many brought casseroles. And hundreds of people prayed. Samuel was mentioned in the Sunday pastoral prayer for weeks, and this was a church of 2000 members. But when our husband and father walked out on us more than a year ago, there were no calls or visits from pastors or others, and no prayer support."[7]

I have also heard women in the church say things like, "I would like to have Mrs. Smith over for dinner, but what would I do with her three boys? I don't have anything here that would entertain them." Usually these women conclude that someone else could do a better job. The problem is that everyone else is thinking the same thing.

Single mothers don't want people to say, "Let's get together sometime." They want to hear, "Can you come for dinner on Friday? Let's set a time right now." Even the most humble meal fixed by someone else can refresh an overworked Mom. There isn't any such thing as a humble meal when it is lovingly served in someone else's home.

When we first moved to this country, we had no relatives on the entire continent. This was a difficult transition for me, because I had grown up in a family-oriented community. But the Lord brought a beautiful married couple into my life, Paul and Florence Turnidge, who adopted me as one of their own.

Paul was part of the maintenance and custodial staff at the Crista Ministries organization. Florence was a full-time homemaker. Together they raised three sons in their very modest house. Although their furniture was made up of bargain buys from garage sales and Salvation Army stores, their home was always comfortably inviting.

In my early years of clinical practice, I used to leave the counseling office utterly exhausted after long eleven-hour days. I carried a very heavy caseload of troubled women and children. The drive home was forty miles, so during the worst winter months, Florence and Paul let me spend weeknights at their home.

I'll never forget the way this couple ministered to me, and I am just one of many who have found refuge in their home. Hundreds of missionaries have stayed with them during their forty-four years of marriage. I still can't figure out how they do so much for others on such a limited income. Florence is the only friend I know who can tell you where to buy turkey for sixty-nine cents a pound all year long. She says, "Food for hurting people is holy stuff."

Florence has a beautiful way of making single mothers feel important. Luncheons are her specialty. She regularly invites one weary mother to her home and creatively dishes up simple meals at a peaceful table. The mother has a captive audience without any distractions. Florence is never bothered by pretentiousness and is perfectly at ease offering whatever is on hand. Even a bowl of soup or a sandwich is delicious when it's accompanied by her tender loving care. Many moms have found new motivation for life around Florence's long, flexible dining table.

The Healing Power of a Sunday School Class

In the chapter on quarreling, I mentioned the story of Dan and Robert, two brothers who had difficulty getting along. Due to brain damage, Dan's attention span was short. This made it hard for him to learn in school. His uncontrollable emotional outbursts also hindered his relationships with other children. Neither he nor they understood why he exploded from time to time.

When he was young, Dan had been taken to a number of Sunday school classes, all of which asked him not to return. The teachers didn't know how to handle his disruptive behavior, so rather than work with him, they closed him out.

When he was in junior high, a baby-sitter took him to a church around the corner from his house. The morning was a disaster. His same antics prevailed, and he caused terrible trouble for the teacher and the other seventh-grade boys.

But this teacher was different. She was very conscientious about her work and determined to love all those boys for the Lord. One Sunday when Dan was absent, she had a heart-to-heart talk with her class. She told the boys that Dan was having problems at home and school and that he needed everyone to love him, not tease him. She asked them to pray for Dan every day.

When Dan returned to class, the boys welcomed him and treated him as if he belonged. In front of the class, the teacher told Dan she knew he was having problems at school and the class wanted to help him. The boys asked him to share his worries so they could pray for him. Believe it or not, Dan began to talk to the whole class. This was the first time he had ever talked openly with anyone about his problems.

Each Sunday Dan gave a progress report to the class, and the class prayed. The teacher also picked Dan up some Saturday mornings and took him out for breakfast.

This had such a tremendous impact on Dan that after an emotional outburst at school he told his teacher, "Please don't ever tell my Sunday school teacher about this. It would really upset her." Dan didn't understand why these explosions occurred, and he rarely felt remorse about them. But something was different this time.

Dan's behavior at church improved each week. He also began making better progress at school. The educational authorities were amazed at his advancement in certain learning skills.

When I told this story recently at a women's conference, a most unusual thing happened. A mother sitting toward the back of the audience stood up and said, "Jean, I must tell you another part of your story. My son was one of the boys in Dan's seventh-grade class. Every Sunday he came home and told the family about Dan so we could pray for him. Dan's name became a common word in our household. For two years we heard progress reports. You will never know how this Sunday school project affected our boy. It taught him concern and compassion and taught our family how to pray together for someone in need." Thanks to one dedicated Sunday school teacher, a little boy from a troubled single-parent family was loved and reached for the Lord. And twelve other little boys experienced the joy of being part of that miracle.

Thinking It Through

1. What do you think about the idea of making an unlovable or unfaithful spouse look good for the children's sake?

2. What can a woman do to help her cope with her feelings about her children's loving her ex-husband's new wife?

3. What can a mother do to protect her children from emotional overload?

4. Everyone needs a balance of input and output. What have you done recently to refresh yourself?

5. What are some creative ways you could refresh a single mother?

6. How, when, and for whom will you do this in the next couple of weeks?

7. What is your church doing to minister to single mothers and their children?

8. What have you learned from this chapter that you can pass on to somebody else?

12

Stepmothering: A Curse or Blessing? ___ ▪▪

The pattern of the American family has drastically changed in the last century. No longer is the average family composed of a mother, father, and two children. These families remain, but surrounding them in great numbers are single-parent families, stepfamilies, and the ghosts of former relationships. The divorce rate in America is close to 50 percent. Eighty percent of these remarry, and 60 percent of these remarriages involve an adult with custody of one or more children. Going into the 1980s, it was estimated that 15 million children lived with a remarried parent.[1] Each year more and more women are becoming stepmothers. For some, this is a blessing, for others, a curse.

Many women remarrying into an existing family have unrealistic expectations of themselves. They feel compelled to keep all the members of their new family happy. They are determined to contradict the wicked stepmother myth and to automatically love their stepchildren. They say, "It's my job to make up to the children for the hurt they suffered from the death of their original family."[2] Unfortunately these expectations are usually reinforced by their partners, relatives, and society.

Mixing Oil With Water

This wasn't the first time I had counseled Mary. We had spent many hours together during her years as a single mother. Now she and Dave were planning to be married.

They had met each other at the church singles' group. Mary and her four children had been abandoned by her husband nearly three years before. Dave and his four children were left alone when his wife decided it was time to make life a full-time party. They hadn't seen her in eighteen months.

During the past year, Mary and Dave found great comfort in their companionship and decided they wanted to spend the rest of their lives together. It seemed the perfect answer to their loneliness. Several camping trips and barbeques with all eight children had convinced them that a new life together would work. I had my doubts.

My suggestions about postponing the wedding plans fell on deaf ears, and within a few months they were husband and wife. Two months after the honeymoon, Mary and Tom were back in my office, completely baffled by the chaos in their home. Mary accused Dave of leaving all the discipline to her and complained of her inability to handle his children. Dave admitted he had been slack in correcting his children. He thought he needed to avoid conflicts with his kids while they were adjusting to living in Mary's house.

Six months later, Mary wished she had never plunged into a second marriage. Dave didn't change and made one excuse after another for his teenagers' outrageous behavior. Both Mary and Dave had gone into the marriage hoping the other would be a strong parent to the entire family. Neither was coping with the pressures.

The children had no interest in blending the families. Dave's children were furious about the change and mobilized as a team ready for battle. His oldest daughter, who acted like a mother to the younger children, was fearful of being demoted to a child again. (Actually this is just what she needed.) Mary tried very hard, but the children were winning the war. One of his children said to me, "You just watch us and see her run!"

Mary's and Dave's children never gave them a chance to develop their marriage relationship. They came into the new family with resistances and were determined to create as many obstacles as possible. Dave's children had never accepted the fact that their mother and father would not get back together. Though their mother had abandoned them, they felt strong bonds with her and denied any hostility toward her. This postponed the expression of their anger for a while, but eventually it burst forth against another object—Mary.

Mary was the enemy. Her intrusion into their lives forced them to mourn the death of their original family. No longer could they deny their feelings. Full-blown anger erupted, and Mary was an easy target. This kind of opposition drained Mary. She dragged to bed each night wondering if it was worth the effort. The constant conflict eventually eroded the marriage.

I wish I could say that all blended families live happily ever after. I wish I could say that if two adults are madly in love, that's enough to make a blended family work. Both are fallacies.

Part of the success of a blended family depends on the children who are included in the marriage circle. All the love in the world between a husband and wife can't make a happy blended family if the children are allowed to ruin it.

I Don't Love My Stepsons!

"I have been married for two years, and my worst fears have come true," Diane complained. "My husband's boys from his previous marriage were dumped on us without warning, and I don't think I can handle it. I've never been around kids before, and all of a sudden I'm an instant mother. I know I want a child of my own someday, but I don't want to raise another woman's hellions!

"I called my mother for some consolation, and all she said was, 'If you love your husband, you will love his boys, too. That's your duty.'

"I don't know what to think. I feel guilty because I don't like the boys, and I'm angry because they've interrupted our lives. My husband keeps saying, 'I never thought you would react like this. Can't you try to enjoy the boys a little? They need a secure home.' "

Diane had a major dilemma. She was a very successful career woman who enjoyed her job. Now she was forced into being a mother before she had fully adjusted to marriage. The boys had stolen the show and become her husband's first priority. They resented sharing their dad with Diane and were compelled to close her out in loyalty to their real mother. No matter what she did, she couldn't win.

When she turned to her mother for help, she got a sermon. "If you are a decent woman, you will love those kids." The truth is, Diane didn't love them, like them, or want them. Her mother's comments did nothing but add to her despair.

As Diane and I talked together, I explained my thoughts about her predicament.

"Diane, as I understand the Bible, I think you have two duties to perform. You are to honor your husband's wishes, and you are to honor his children. Honoring implies positive intentions and actions. It has nothing to do with personal feelings. It would be ridiculous for you to think you can automatically love two children who came crashing into your life. They have changed everything. I know you can't help feeling angry, but you can govern your actions toward the boys. You must separate your feelings from your behavior."

She wasn't sure she could do that, so I took the conversation one step further. "Let me ask you a question. Are there people on your staff at work who you don't like?"

"Of course."

"Do you respond differently to them than to those you like?"

"No. That wouldn't be professional. I'd never have the job I'm in, if I allowed feelings to guide my responses."

"I agree with you," I added. "I think you will understand what I'm going to say now. The only way you are going to survive your marriage is to use professional tactics in the new job that has been dumped on you. Look at the two boys as a new work responsibility that you never requested. Imagine that you warned the boss you didn't have the training or experience to handle this kind of work, and that you were already overloaded. You made it clear that you couldn't do it, but you didn't tell him you wouldn't do it because that would be insubordination and might mean a termination notice. Commit yourself to doing the job regardless of your feelings. Don't feel guilty about not loving them. Monitor your reactions and do the best you can. Believe me, ordinary mothers don't feel a lot of sentimental love toward their children all the time. Periodically they may not even like them. Rest assured, you're not alone in your frustrations."

Seven years have passed since Diane heard this advice. Today she continues to be a stepmother of two sons and is the natural mother of two daughters. The adjustments have been made. The first two years were difficult, but she was determined to succeed in her "new work responsibilities." Looking at the family today, you would never know that some of the kids were "his" and some were "theirs." Diane accomplished her job with flair.

From Ellen's Journal

A plane goes down in the Cascade mountains. Dave's plane is missing. The descriptions match. My childhood

sweetheart and husband of eighteen years is gone. Pain
... hurt ... tears. I'm left alone with three young
children.

A new life must begin. I'm responsible now. I must earn
a living. University classes start today. Go to school ...
study ... cry ... study ... cry. I don't want this
responsibility, Lord! It's too much, too heavy.

My friend's sister died. I wrote a letter of sympathy to
her husband and children. I had almost forgotten about it,
but then came a knock at my door. "Hello. I'm Karl. You
wrote me a letter when my wife died." Instant empathy.
He's looking ahead. I'm still looking back. I must press
forward. What's over is over.

More dates with Karl. Companionship. Attraction. Embarrassment over being seen with another man. Secrets.
Excitement. I don't know how to think.

Karl said, "I love you!" today.

"Don't say that yet. You can't know in such a short
time."

"I love you. Will you marry me?"

I'm not sure I can be a good mother to seven children.
Seven children! "Yes, Karl, I will marry you."

The wedding, the honeymoon in Hawaii, then home to
seven beautiful children, ages nine to fifteen. Adjustments.
Hurts. Tears. It's difficult for the kids to say "Mom" and
"Dad" and "Brother" and "Sister."

The two oldest children from our families vie for position. There can only be one oldest in the family now.

I feel like I'm failing with Richard (my oldest stepson).
He keeps pulling away from everyone.

Choose to love. Care. Build a new life.

Lord, I think we are going to make it.

Was my prediction premature?

Karl had chest pains at 12:30 A.M. Cold, clammy sweat.
Aid arrived. "Your husband has had a heart attack."

"Karl, you can't die! We've only had six months of

marriage together. Crucial months. Maturing months. I'm learning how to love again."

The doctor says he's going to make it. Karl is home.

No improvement. Now the doctor says he has less than two years to live.

No, God! No! No! No!

"Karl. You have less than a year. We are going to Hawaii."

Hawaii is beautiful.

"Karl, I've learned to love you in such a short time, to lean and depend on you. Karl, you can't leave me alone. I won't let you."

Today Karl said, "I didn't think you could handle the children at first, but now I know you can do it."

No, Karl. You can't do this to me. No, no, no!

Shortly after affirming Ellen, Karl died. To this day, Ellen is a single mother parenting seven children, four of Karl's and three of her own. She has survived the death of two husbands and with the Lord's help has successfully blended two families. But the blending didn't come easily. It has taken years of hard work.

When it seemed her world was crumbling, structure helped bring some semblance of order. Ellen made it a habit to attend church with the children each Sunday. They rode in one car and sang on the way to services. Once a month she met with her pastor and his wife. They talked and prayed about the children, and she received advice about household fix-it jobs.

Each child has a special time alone with Ellen during the week. Some chose to take walks; others liked to go out for breakfast. "There wasn't enough of me to go around. Never enough time," Ellen said. "Though I tried to meet regularly with each child, sometimes I resented having seven of them. I had to make so many decisions, especially about limits.

"It wasn't easy to be firm about the rules. I hated being

the only one to say no. Time and again I knelt beside my bed and asked God to help me not back down to the children. It was amazing how these prayer sessions helped. Somehow, He always gave me the strength to keep going."

Time alone helped, too. Ellen walked, bicycled, or swam several times a week. The exercise gave her a break from the children and a chance to treat herself with kindness.

Family support was essential. Ellen's parents lived with her and the children a couple of months each winter. Ellen also kept in close contact with her stepchildren's extended families. She hosted birthday parties and other family gatherings with their grandparents and cousins. Occasionally the children visited relatives for two to three days, and everyone enjoyed the change of pace.

Ellen also looked to the schools for additional assistance. The six younger children were very active in their small Christian school. Several of the male teachers were good father figures. School activities were special family outings. Those who were not playing basketball or performing in the plays sat in the audience rooting for the others. Afterwards, Ellen treated them to their favorite snack.

Reflecting on the years since Karl's death, Ellen readily admits life hasn't been easy. But she also boasts of God's ability to restore and redeem: "People ask me about the good things that have come out of our losses. God has become our intimate companion, who gives us daily strength to look forward. The eight of us are more sensitive, understanding, and less judgmental of others who suffer. I have learned the needs of single women and can minister to them with empathy now.

"The kids say our blended family has taught them how to cooperate with others. They had to learn to love others in spite of differences. This helped their adjustments with college roommates, marriage partners, and work companions. Today they are mature young adults who don't expect everything to go their own way.

"The deaths of my young husbands taught us a lesson in vulnerability. Karl and Dave's absence reminded other fathers to spend time with their families and initiated conversations about finances, wills, and so forth. Since we can only count on the present, we need to make the most of today and enjoy one another *now*."

Guidelines for Parents of Blended Families

Years ago, I did premarital counseling for couples planning second marriages. Many of them felt they should lay down rigid guidelines for their children and enforce them immediately after the honeymoon. They were certain that somebody, somewhere, had devised a list of rules that would ensure success.

Unfortunately there is no magic list, and a rigid set of *do*s and *don't*s for a new family tends to cause more trouble than it's worth. But there are a few tools I've seen work very well in blended families.

Guidelines for Mom and Dad

- Top priority is for the new mom and dad to have private times together. It's almost more important than in a first marriage, because there the marriage preceded the children, but in a second marriage, the children came first. You are not betraying your children by investing in your mate. You are protecting them from another marriage loss.
- Don't be hard on yourself for not loving your stepchildren. Act correctly, even when you don't feel right. Good feelings usually follow good actions.
- Carve out a role for yourself as a stepparent that is different from and does not compete with the natural parents.
- Give stepchildren plenty of time alone with their real

parent. Don't push for full family activities all the time.

- For the first two years after the marriage, each natural parent should take responsibility for disciplining his own children. I realize this can cause problems if a couple doesn't agree on limits and consequences. For example, a stepmother may think the children should report home before dark for safety reasons, whereas the husband thinks his boys should have more freedom. What if the boys from both sides are the same age?

- I still think a mother can expect certain things from her own children and leave the parenting of her husband's children to him. Even though things may get sticky, this standard leads to better solutions than any other method I've seen. Too many times boys become absolutely defiant when their stepmother tries to discipline them. If they have any anger about the remarriage, it is much safer for them to take it out on their "wicked stepmom" than to dump it on their father. The new mom is likely to hear, "You're not my mother, so butt out!"

- If you are a stepmother, you need breaks for yourself! Mental fatigue comes from the added strains of stepmothering, and you need personal time and space to assert your identity apart from the larger family.

- Avoid becoming highly emotional or overinvolved. Sometimes you need to *back off*. You can't always straighten out everyone in the household.

- Take an interest in your stepchildren's hobbies. Be active in their school life and available to assist them.

- Accept their friends and invite them home.

- Be gracious to their grandparents. Expect them to be on guard with you and possibly antagonistic. Keep being courteous. Caring relationships with relatives take time to evolve.

- When appropriate, cooperate with their biological mother.

- After your stepchildren have been with their biological mother, allow for a reentry period. They may have trouble getting back into the swing of things. Expect them to be angry and do things that irritate you right after they return.

Guidelines for the Family

- Have realistic expectations. Life is not going to be easy for a while. When families are blended, there is an adjustment period of two to three years. In some cases, it may take longer. Don't be surprised if, after entering your family, the children drag out all their worst behavior and perhaps some surprising new behavior, to see how much they can get away with. Don't panic and think they are worse than before. They are simply trying to "feel their way" into a new life.
- It's difficult to have new people move into your territory, and it's hard being the new member in a preexisting group. Territorial problems can be diminished by starting out in a new home. There are fewer haunting memories and everyone begins on neutral ground.
- Set aside family nights for games and play.
- Meet together as a family at specific times to share ideas about discipline. Let the children suggest suitable punishments. The penalties will seem fairer to them if they choose them. The family forum is also a good place to verbalize feelings of anger and resentment and define constructive ways of handling these emotions.
- Hold family devotions. Prayer may change hostile attitudes better than anything else.
- Visiting children usually feel like outsiders. It may help to set aside a special "space" just for them when they come. Even a corner of a room or a dresser drawer for their belongings can make them feel more welcome.
- If life gets too complicated, seek professional counseling for the family.
- Don't give up. The first two years after remarriage may be the toughest time in your life. Your feelings will be hurt now and then. But despite the initial hardships, a

second marriage can be wonderful. I have heard many women say, "My second marriage has brought great healing and many new beginnings into my life. It has been worth all the effort."

Parenting is one of the most difficult, demanding, and frustrating jobs a person ever undertakes. Stepparenting is even harder. There are no hard and fast rules that insure successful blending. A great deal of time must be allowed for new families to work things out. But the rewards can be terrific. One stepmother told me, "I'm closer to my stepdaughter than I am to my own two children. It's like we are best friends." Another stepmother said, "I get a warm feeling when I get a birthday card from my kids. But when a birthday card comes from one of my stepchildren, I get a warm feeling and something else besides. Our relationship is very special because we created it."[3]

All life experiences, positive and negative, can cause growth. Stepparenting definitely increases a person's flexibility, empathy, and understanding of the human condition. It can also give you a glimpse at your personal resources and ability to care for someone else's children. Great joy comes from seeing the Lord use you as a tool to help Him heal the wounds others have suffered. Perhaps this is part of what Christ meant when He said, "Greater love has no one than this, that one lay down his life for his friends" (John 15:13 NAS).

The following publications contain additional information on stepparenting that you may find useful.

Bohannan, Paul J., and Rosemary J. Erickson. "Stepping In." *Psychology Today*, January, 1978.

Bustanoby, Andre. *The Ready Made Family.* Grand Rapids: Zondervan, 1982.

Frydenger, Adrienne and Tom. *The Blended Family.* Old Tappan, N.J.: Fleming H. Revell Co., 1984.

Juroe, David and Bonnie. *Successful Step Parenting.* Old Tappan, N.J.: Fleming H. Revell Co., 1982.

Maddox, Brenda. *The Half Parent.* New York: Evans, 1975.

Noble, June and William. *How to Live With Other People's Children.* New York: Hawthorne Books, 1977.

Reingold, Carmel Berman. *Remarriage.* New York: Harper & Row, 1976.

Spann, Owen and Nancie. *Your Child? I Thought It Was My Child.* Pasadena: Ward Ritchie Press, 1977.

Visher, Emily and John. *Step Families.* New York: Lyle Stuart, 1980.

Thinking It Through

1. Mary and Dave's attempt at blending their families didn't work. Discuss possible reasons for the deterioration of their relationships.

2. Diane had a tough role to play. How would you react if two boys were dumped on you without warning?

3. What kind of counsel would you give someone who is faced with a predicament similar to Diane's?

13

What About Moral Values? ▪

Are values changing? Some say yes, and the changes in many ways are not positive. One retired schoolteacher said, "Twenty years ago if a student was caught cheating, it was embarrassing to the student. The student didn't want his peers to know. Last year when I caught a boy cheating, his reply was, 'You didn't tell me I couldn't cheat!' "

William J. Bennett, secretary of education, has said that Americans want schools to do two things: Teach our children to speak, think, write, and count; and help them develop standards of right and wrong to guide them through life.[1]

While some claim that it is important to form character at school, others claim it can't be done. Bennett says, "Some educators deliberately avoid questions of right and wrong or remain neutral about them. Many have turned to values education theories that seek to guide children in developing their own values by discussion, dialogue and simulation—a tragically mistaken approach, since research indicates that it has had no discernible effect on children's behavior. At best, this misguided method threatens to leave our children morally adrift."[2]

If Americans agree there is a profound need for moral development among children, how can this be accomplished? First, we must look to the home for some answers. One of the most important tasks of parenting is guiding children through moral development. Dr. Thomas Likona says, "Most parents want their children to be intelligent, talented, and attractive. These nice things add to the lives of children, yet if they do not possess all of these qualities, they can still 'stand tall' as human beings. If, however, they are not good, decent people, can they 'stand tall?' "[3] My answer to this question is, "Probably not."

I have talked with scores of mothers who have asked me, "How can I raise my son to be a man's man and at the same time help him develop tenderness and compassion toward others?" or "How can I nurture a competitive drive in my boy and at the same time guard him from becoming too power hungry?"

The Stages of Moral Development

For over a dozen years, psychologist Lawrence Kohlberg followed the development of moral knowledge among seventy-five boys in the United States and observed moral knowledge in other cultures as a comparison with his sample. Based on his findings, Kohlberg says moral development occurs in three major states: preconventional morality, conventional morality, and postconventional (or autonomous) morality.

Kohlberg believes preconventional-stage children are guided by pleasure, pain, and the satisfaction of their own needs. They respond primarily to punishment and reward. This first stage occurs from birth to age twelve.[4]

During this phase of development, parents must consistently teach their children what is right and wrong in relation to their wants. For example, most two-year-olds like to explore driveways, sidewalks, and streets. If one ventures out into a parkway, the parent naturally tries to catch the child and say, "Johnny, that's a no-no. If you go out in the street, you might get hit by a car!" The two-year-old concludes a "no-no" is wrong and everything else is okay.

After the age of six, most children think in terms of what they can give and get in a situation. They obey for the sake of winning a reward. It is very important for parents to consistently follow through with promised rewards. If they don't, they send their children mixed signals. Double messages dangerously confuse children. I've seen too many little boys totally throw out their parents' rules because obedience didn't get them what they were promised.

In the next stage, conventional morality, Kohlberg says children judge their actions in terms of being good and respecting authority. The child moves beyond himself to consider his family, peers, and the world at large. His moral choices are based on guilt and peer pressures. This phase takes place between twelve and twenty years of age.[5]

The young adolescent is moving into a period of life when he begins saying to himself, "I should or shouldn't do this or that." He has a sense of right and wrong based on what he has been taught in his family and among his peers. Having shaped his sense of right and wrong in younger years, parents must consistently support his good moral choices in the teen years. An adolescent needs to hear his parents say, "I am proud of you for making a good choice" or "I am disappointed in your poor choice." He also needs to understand *why* his parents think his choice was right or wrong. This helps him internalize standards and paves the way for him to move into the third stage of moral development.

Kohlberg's final stage of moral development, autonomous morality, occurs in adulthood, if at all. In this stage the individual tries to find general principles to govern his actions and the actions of others. He internalizes morals for himself, develops selfless concern for others, and is conscious of his rights and responsibilities in society. In Kohlberg's multicultural study, very few subjects ever reached this stage of moral development.[6]

The big question here is: Where will the child get his standards? For Christian parents, the answer is obvious: Biblical principles become the guide and building blocks for moral attitudes and conduct.

Building a Godly Moral Foundation

Christian parents have a challenging job. Nearly everywhere their children go, they are exposed to anti-Christian beliefs. We live in a very complex society that does not promote biblical morals. Television, music, and the media pump children full of information that is anything but Christian. The prevailing philosophies of this age are: "Look out for number one. You only live once, so grab all the gusto you can get. If it feels good, do it!"

What can Christian parents do to counteract these values and build a godly moral foundation for their children? The following suggestions can provide a start.

Clarify your own values. Before parents can develop morals in their children, they need to define their own values. What is important to you? Whatever you value, your children will value. What do you want for your children?

Most parents desire their children to be fair, honest, and trustworthy. They want them to know about kindness and compassion and their opposites. They want them to respect the rights of others and feel a reasonable measure of concern for their fellowman. They want them to recognize greed and overreaching ambition, as well as know that hard work pays off. These are godly values.

Help children demonstrate your values. If you want your son to grow up to be considerate and respectful of women, teach him to act considerate as a child. Have him hold the car door for his mother and sisters. Show him how to assist them with their coats, seat them at a table, and not start shoveling food until the hostess has taken her first bite.

If you want your son to become a man who brings happiness to others, give him opportunities to do this while he is growing up. Beth used to make a big deal about her birthday and Mother's Day. About a month before the celebrations, she began saying things to her children like, "I can't wait for that wonderful birthday cake and all the cards." I was a bit bewildered by her actions, because they were so foreign to her usual unselfish attitude. One afternoon my daughter asked her why she made such a fuss over her birthday. I've never forgotten her reply. She said, "To be honest, I don't care a bit about my own birthday. And you know I have never been a cake eater. But I want my boys to learn to be considerate and honor others. If I teach them to honor me on occasions like this, maybe they'll think of others when they're adults."

Beth also insisted her boys visit their grandparents and take presents or baked goodies to them on holidays and birthdays. She said, "I can't make them feel tenderness toward others, but I can help them demonstrate acts of caring. If I don't take the lead and show enthusiasm about bringing happiness to others, why should they ever bother?" Sometimes her boys didn't care for the fuss over family birthdays (when it wasn't their own), but Beth didn't back down. She kept telling herself, "Someday, the push will pay off."

And it did. The last time Beth and I talked, she told me one of her sons was engaged. A few weeks before, his fiancée had completed a hard year of school, and he sent her a huge bunch of red roses. That was quite a sacrifice for a young man on a limited budget, and proof that Beth had accomplished one of her goals.

When her boys were young, the senior pastor of her large church requested to see the boys individually. Every six months they "reported in" about their behavior and told how they were honoring their single mother. Beth didn't always know what was said in the meetings, but she said they made a tremendous impression on her boys and reminded them of their accountability to others.

Beth creatively taught her sons to bring happiness to others. Another mother inspired her son to serve with his talents. For several years I have admired a brilliant young medical surgeon who lives near us. He excels in everything he does. His mother says he never gave her any problems while growing up, and his wife adores him. His friends and acquaintances say he is one of the finest people they know.

I talked with Jack recently, and asked him, "Why are you such a giant of a man? Everyone who knows you boasts of your greatness."

He told me something about his mother that intrigued me. When he was a young man, she taught Jack that he had superior gifts. His IQ was on a genius level; that was apparent to everyone. He was also unusually strong and handsome. Jack said his mother told him, "Since you have many gifts, you have an obligation to be great, honest, and to serve mankind. You have not earned these gifts. They were given to you. What you are on the inside must be as superior as the talents that show on the outside." To this day, those words ring in his ears and motivate him to excel in his work and relationships.

Lorraine, a mother of three children, wanted her children to honor Sunday as a family day. She said, "My husband and I felt Sunday should be a peaceful time for our family to be togther. But somehow it always turned into a day full of noise and commotion, the same as any other busy day. Steve and I decided we needed to be more passionate about sticking to our convictions and decided to make some drastic changes. We told the children that

Sunday was to be strictly a family day. No playmates were allowed to come over, and the children were not to leave the house unless the family went together."

Lorraine was amazed at the effect this had on their family. Everyone slowed down, read more books, communicated more, and became better friends with one another. Now she says, "As parents, we need to fight for our values. Once we decide something is important, we must work hard to give those values high priority."

Be an example. Morals are better caught than taught. The best way to pass on values to your children is through living them. As one father put it, "You've got to *be* it, not just talk it." If you want your children to show respect for others, treat them with respect. Listen without interrupting. Use "please" and "thank you." Walk alongside them, not ten yards ahead.

Andrew Murray, one of the greatest Christian writers of the past one hundred years, was a father of a large family and preached many sermons about raising children. He quotes the proverb, "Train up a child in the way which he should go . . ." and says, "Training comes far more through example than precept. The atmosphere of a well-regulated home and the influence of self-control exhibited by parents unconsciously set their mark on a child. When parents give way to impulse and temper, perhaps at the time when reproving or restraining the child's temper, the effect of their good advice is more than neutralized."[7]

When parents model moral behavior for their children, they need to keep in mind that attitudes are just as contagious as actions. If I make my children go to church, read the Bible, and pray, but don't demonstrate my love for church, reading my Bible, and praying, I might be doing more harm than good. They may learn a legalistic list of *do*s and *don't*s rather than develop a personal love for God.

A parent's words must also agree with his actions. If

you want your children to be generous, don't pass up opportunities to put something in the offering plate or give love offerings to the needy. If you want your children to share the Lord with their friends at school, talk about Christ with your neighbors and friends who don't know Him. If you want your children to forgive others, you must forgive and ask them for forgiveness when you make mistakes. If you want your children to be free of prejudice, they must see you extend yourself to those of different races and colors. If you want your children to be truthful, don't take home the excess change the grocer gives you. Instead, use the incident as a chance to teach them that honesty is more important than an extra $10 bill.

Encourage your children to develop their thinking skills. When moral dilemmas arise, ask them questions like, "What is the problem? What happened to you because of your behavior? What happened to others? What other choices did you have?"

You can also help them learn how to think by reading stories with a moral message. When characters are forced to make a moral choice, stop the story and ask your children what they would do if they were in the same situation. Find out why they would make that choice, and then help them look at their decision in light of God's Word.

Educate your children by telling them what you believe and why. Most of us make statements like, "My mom used to say . . ." or "My father always emphasized. . . ." A young doctor I admire told me he spent many days with his grandparents while he was growing up. He thought they were magnificent people with very high standards. In everything he did, he wanted to please them. When I asked him if he had urges to cheat in school, as many boys do, he said, "I could never have cheated, because I knew it was totally against my grandparents' beliefs, and it would hurt them too much." Children need to hear their elders talk about their beliefs.

Pray for your children. One of the greatest tools parents can use for shaping their children's liv̲s is intercessory prayer. If we want our children to cling to godly values, we must pray not only for their physical and emotional development, but also for their spiritual progress. In today's society, it isn't enough for parents to simply be good examples. They must go a step further and call on God to guide and protect their children, to buffer the ungodly influences that press in on them, to accomplish His purposes in their lives, and to enable them by His Spirit to live according to the guidelines they have learned at home. God says, "Call to Me, and I will answer you, and I will tell you great and mighty things, which you do not know" (Jeremiah 33:3 NAS). "The prayer of a righteous man is powerful and effective" (James 5:16 NIV).

Assisting children in their moral development is not an easy task. It requires parents to live close to the Lord and to lean on Him for divine understanding and guidance. Andrew Murray once said to a group of parents, "No grace of the Christian life is obtained without sacrifice; parenting, or the influencing and forming other souls for God, needs special self-sacrifice. Like every difficult work, it needs purpose, attention and perseverance. . . . Our duty as parents is never measured by what we feel is within our power to do, but by what God's grace makes possible for us. And we cannot know fully what grace can enable us to do, until we begin."[8] The good news is, when we're helping our children develop godly morals, we can rest assured that God is always eager to assist us with His supernatural resources.

Thinking It Through

1. Is it your opinion that values are changing? Explain.

2. Have your children's teachers remained neutral about defining right and wrong in the classroom?

3. How do you reward your children for their good choices?

4. How do you handle your children when they make poor choices?

5. List your five top values.

6. How do you help your children demonstrate your values?

7. Tell about an incident when you were a good role model for your child.

8. What are some ways you can help your children develop their thinking skills?

9. What do you usually pray about concerning your children?

10. What have you learned from this chapter that you can share with one other person this week? Decide when and with whom you will do this.

Appendix 1
Resources on
Sexual Development ⸻ ▪▪

A Boy Today. . . .A Man Tomorrow. Basic facts about puberty, sexuality, reproductive health. Booklet for pre-teen, young teen boys. Write: Optimistic International, 4494 Lindell Boulevard, St. Louis, MO 63108.

How to Talk to Your Child About Sex: A Guide for Parents. Guidelines for communication, especially with young children. Write: The National PTA, 700 North Rush Street, Chicago, IL 60611-2571.

How Your Child Learns About Sex. Discussion of sexual development of children, parental influences on attitudes and behavior, answers to common questions. Write: Ross Laboratories, Columbus, OH 43216.

Sex Education: The Parents' Role. Guidelines for communication, common questions of children. Write: RAJ Publication, P.O. Box 15720, Lakewood, CO 80215.

Talking to Preteenagers About Sex. Facts about physical and emotional development, common concerns of parents. Write: Public Affairs Pamphlets, 381 Park Avenue South, New York, NY 10016.

Talking With Your Young Child About Sex. Guide to early psychosexual development, common concerns, strategies for communication. Write: Network Publications, P.O. Box 1830, Santa Cruz, CA 95061-1830.

Teaching Your Child About Sexuality. Guide to sexual development, strategies for communication. Write: ACOG, Suite 300 East, 600 Maryland Avenue SW, Washington, D.C. 20024-2588.

Deciding About Sex . . . The Choice to Abstain. Suggestions about decision making, responsible behavior, saying no. Contemporary format pamphlet for young and midteens. Write: Network Publications, P.O. Box 1830, Santa Cruz, CA 95061-1830.

Many Teens Are Saying "No." Basic facts about sexuality, feelings, relationships, pressures, decision making. Pamphlet for all teens. Write: U.S. Government Printing Office, Washington, D.C. 20402.

Appendix 2
Work Responsibilities
for Children ▪▪

Ages Two to Four

1. Pick up unused toys and put in the proper place.
2. Put books and magazines in a rack.
3. Sweep the floor.
4. Place napkins, plates, and silverware on the table.
5. Clean up what they drop after eating.
6. Choose between two foods at breakfast. Learn to make simple decisions.
7. Clear own place at the table. Put the dishes on the counter after clearing the leftovers off the plate.
8. Toilet training.
9. Simple hygiene—brush teeth, wash and dry hands and face, and brush hair.
10. Undress self—dress with some help.
11. Wipe up own accidents.
12. Carry boxed or canned goods from the grocery sacks to the proper shelf.

Ages Four to Five

1. Set the table.
2. Put the groceries away.
3. Help with grocery shopping and compile a grocery list.
4. Polish shoes and clean up afterwards.
5. Follow a schedule for feeding pets.
6. Help do yard and garden work.
7. Help make the beds and vacuum.
8. Help do the dishes or fill the dishwasher.
9. Dust the furniture.
10. Spread butter on sandwiches.
11. Prepare cold cereal.
12. Help mother prepare plates of food for the family dinner.
13. Make a simple dessert (add topping to cupcakes, pour the toppings on ice cream).
14. Hold the hand mixer to whip potatoes or mix up a cake.
15. Share toys with friends (practice courtesy).
16. Get the mail.
17. Tell parent his whereabouts before going out to play.
18. Play without constant adult supervision and attention.
19. Bring in the milk from the milk box.
20. Hang socks, handkerchiefs, and washcloths on a low line.
21. Polish silver.
22. Polish car.
23. Sharpen pencils.

Ages Five to Six

1. Help with the meal planning and grocery shopping.
2. Make own sandwich or simple breakfast, then clean up.

3. Pour own drink.
4. Prepare the dinner table.
5. Tear up lettuce for the salad.
6. Put certain ingredients into a recipe.
7. Make bed and clean room.
8. Dress on own and choose outfit for the day.
9. Scrub the sink, toilet, and bathtub.
10. Clean mirrors and windows.
11. Separate clothing for washing.
12. Fold clean clothes and put them away.
13. Answer the telephone and begin to dial the phone.
14. Yardwork.
15. Pay for small purchases.
16. Help clean out the car.
17. Take out the garbage.
18. Decide how he wants to spend his share of the family entertainment fund.
19. Feed his pets and clean the living area.
20. Learn to tie shoes.

First Grade

1. Choose own clothing for the day.
2. Shake rugs.
3. Water plants and flowers.
4. Peel vegetables.
5. Cook simple food (hot dogs, boiled eggs, and toast).
6. Prepare own school lunch.
7. Help hang clothes on the clothesline.
8. Hang up own clothes in the closet.
9. Gather wood for the fireplace.
10. Rake leaves and weed.
11. Take pet for walk.
12. Tie own shoes.
13. Care for his own minor injuries.
14. Keep the garbage container clean.

15. Clean out inside of car.
16. Straighten or clean out silverware drawer.

Second Grade

1. Oil and care for bike.
2. Take phone messages.
3. Run errands for parents.
4. Sweep and wash patio area.
5. Water the lawn.
6. Wash dog or cat.
7. Train pets.
8. Carry in the grocery sacks.
9. Get self up in the morning and go to bed at night on own.
10. Learn to be polite, courteous, and to share; respect others.
11. Carry own lunch money and notes back to school.
12. Leave the bathroom in order.
13. Do simple ironing.
14. Wash down walls and scrub floors.

Third Grade

1. Fold napkins properly and set silverware properly.
2. Mop or buff the floor.
3. Clean blinds.
4. Help rearrange furniture. Help plan the layout.
5. Run own bathwater.
6. Help others with their work when asked.
7. Straighten own closet and drawers.
8. Shop for and select own clothing and shoes with parent.
9. Change school clothes without being told.
10. Fold blankets.
11. Sew buttons.
12. Sew rips in seams.

13. Clean storage room.
14. Clean up animal "messes" in the yard and house.
15. Begin to read recipes and cook for the family.
16. Cut flowers and make a centerpiece.
17. Pick fruit off trees.
18. Build a campfire, get items ready to cook out (charcoal, hamburgers).
19. Paint fence or shelves.
20. Help write simple letters.
21. Write thank-you notes.
22. Help with defrosting and cleaning the refrigerator.
23. Feed the baby.
24. Polish silverware, copper, or brass items.
25. Clean patio furniture.
26. Wax living room furniture.

Fourth Grade

1. Change sheets and put dirty sheets in hamper.
2. Operate the washer or the dryer.
3. Measure detergent.
4. Buy groceries using a list and comparative shopping.
5. Cross streets unassisted.
6. Keep own appointments.
7. Prepare pastries from mixes.
8. Prepare a family meal.
9. Receive and answer own mail.
10. Pour and make tea, coffee, and instant drinks.
11. Wait on guests.
12. Plan own birthday.
13. Simple first aid.
14. Do neighborhood chores.
15. Sew, knit, or weave (even using a sewing machine).
16. Do chores without a reminder.
17. Learn banking and to be thrifty and trustworthy.
18. Wash the family car.

Fifth Grade

1. Be alone at home for short periods.
2. Handle sums of money up to $5.00.
3. Take the city bus to selected destinations.
4. Proper conduct when staying overnight with a friend. Pack own suitcase.
5. Responsible for personal hobby.
6. Handle self properly when in public places alone or with peers.

Sixth Grade

1. Join outside organizations, do assignments, and attend. Able to take responsibility as a leader.
2. Put siblings to bed and dress them.
3. Clean pool and pool area.
4. Respect others' property.
5. Run own errands.
6. Mow lawn with supervision.
7. Help Father build things and do family errands.
8. Schedule himself time for studies.
9. Buy own sweets or treats.
10. Responsible for a paper route.
11. Check and add oil to car under supervision.

Junior High

1. Determine how late he should stay up during the week. Also determine how late he should be out for evening gatherings (through mutual parent-child discussion and agreement).
2. Responsibility for preparing family meals.
3. Social awareness: good health, exercise, necessary rest, correct weight, nutritious food, physical examinations.
4. Anticipate the needs of others and initiate the appropriate action.

5. Acceptance of capabilities and limitations.
6. Self-respect or individual worth.
7. Responsibility for one's decisions.
8. Mutual respect, loyalty, and honesty in the family.

Notes ■

Chapter one

1. Booker T. Washington, *Up From Slavery* (Norwalk, Conn.: The Heritage Press, 1970), 20.
2. Louis B. Harlan, *Booker T. Washington, The Wizard of Tuskegee*, vol. 2 (New York: Oxford University Press, 1983), 3.
3. Ralph G. Martin, *The Life of Lady Randolph Churchill* (New York: New American Library, 1969), 247.
4. Ibid., 245.
5. Ibid., 246.
6. Ibid., 164.
7. Ibid., 296.
8. Rebecca Lamar Harmon, *Susannah, Mother of the Wesleys* (Nashville: Pantheon Press, 1978), 163.
9. Skevington A. Wood, *The Burning Heart* (Grand Rapids: Wm. B. Eerdmans, 1967), 73.
10. Harmon, *Susannah*, 140.
11. Ibid., 55–63.
12. Ibid., 163.

Chapter two

1. Benjamin Spock, *Baby and Child Care*, rev. ed. (New York: Simon and Schuster, 1976), 39.
2. Ibid., 394.
3. Arnold Gesell, Francis Ilg, and Louise Bates Ames, *Infant and Child in the Culture of Today* (New York: Harper & Row, 1974).
4. Spock, *Baby and Child Care*, 398.
5. Ibid., 402.
6. Ibid., 403.
7. Spurgeon O. English and Stuart M. Finch, *Introduction to Psychiatry* (New York: W. W. Norton & Co., 1957), 25.
8. Spock, *Baby and Child Care*, 431.
9. Ibid.

Chapter three

1. *See* Arnold Gesell, Frances Ilg, and Louis Bates, *Youth: The Years From Ten to Sixteen* (New York: Harper and Brothers, 1956), 83.
2. Benjamin Spock, *Baby and Child Care* (New York: Simon and Schuster, 1976), 466.
3. Ibid., 471.

Chapter four

1. Harvey Kaufman, University of Washington Medical School lectures, 1961–1962.
2. Benjamin Spock, *Baby and Child Care* (New York: Simon and Schuster, 1976), 466.
3. Ibid., 464.
4. Arnold Gesell, Frances Ilg, and Louise Bates, *Youth: The Years From Ten to Sixteen* (New York: Harper and Brothers, 1956), 139.
5. Ibid., 175.

Chapter five

1. Wardell B. Pomeroy, *Boys and Sex* (New York: Dell, 1981), 30.
2. Ibid., 32.
3. Spurgeon O. English and Stuart M. Finch, *Introduction to Psychiatry* (New York: W. W. Norton, 1957), 127.
4. Ibid., 127, 128.
5. Harry Bakwin and Ruth Morris Bakwin, *Clinical Management and Behavior Disorders in Children* (Philadelphia and London: W. B. Saunders Co., 1967), 429.
6. James Dobson, *How to Build Self-Esteem in Your Child* (Old Tappan, N.J.: Fleming H. Revell Co., 1974), 74.
7. Peter Wyden and Barbara Wyden, *Growing Up Straight* (New York: New American Library, 1968), 49.

Chapter six

1. C. A. Tripp, *The Homosexual Matrix* (New York: McGraw-Hill, 1975), 80.
2. Alfred Kinsey, *Sexual Behavior in the Human Male* (Philadelphia: W. B. Saunders Co., 1948), 216–218.
3. Albert Ellis, *Homosexuality* (New York: Lyle Stuart, 1965), 50.
4. Ibid.
5. Wardell B. Pomeroy, *Boys and Sex* (New York: Dell, 1981), 5.
6. Peter Wyden and Barbara Wyden, *Growing Up Straight* (New York: New American Library, 1968), 86.
7. Howard Brown, *Familiar Faces, Hidden Lives* (New York and London: Harcourt Brace Jovanovich, 1975), 172.
8. Edward A. Strecker, *Their Mother's Sons* (New York: J. B. Lippincott, 1946), 129.
9. Tripp, *Homosexual Matrix*, 83.
10. Brown, *Familiar Faces*, 84.
11. Wyden, *Growing Up*, 50.
12. Kinsey, *Sexual Behavior*, 54.

13. Brown, *Familiar Faces*, 33.
14. Strecker, *Their Mother's Sons*, 21.
15. Wyden, *Growing Up*, 41.
16. Neil Heilbrun, University of Washington Medical School lectures, 1961–1962.

Chapter eight

1. Louise Bates Ames, *He Hit Me First* (New York: Red Dembner Enterprises, 1982), 18.
2. James Dobson, *Dr. Dobson Answers Your Questions* (Wheaton, Ill.: Tyndale House, 1982), 222.
3. Ibid.
4. Ibid., 220.

Chapter nine

1. J. Allan Petersen, "Raising Kids in an Unhappy Marriage," in Jay Kesler, *Parents and Teenagers* (Wheaton, Ill.: Scripture Press, 1986), 130.
2. Ibid., 131.
3. Edward A. Strecker, *Their Mother's Sons* (New York: J. B. Lippincott, 1946), 185.
4. Ibid., 197.
5. Ibid., 198.
6. Harvey Kaufman, University of Washington Medical School lectures, 1961–1962.
7. Strecker, *Their Mother's Sons*, 211.

Chapter eleven

1. Benjamin Spock, *Problems of Parents* (Boston: Houghton Mifflin/Riverside Press, 1962), 223.
2. Ibid., 224.
3. Ellen Goodman, "Families Aren't What They Were in the Beavers' Day," Everett *Herald* (January 26, 1988), 9A.

4. Brenda Wilbee, "Part of the Family," *Moody Monthly*, vol. 88, no. 2 (October 1987), 18.
5. Ibid.
6. Ibid., 19.
7. David Lambert, "Coming Up Short," *Moody Monthly*, vol. 88, no. 2 (October 1987), 19.

Chapter twelve

1. Emily Visher and John Visher, *Step-Families* (New York: Brunner/Mazel, 1979), 18.
2. Ibid., 50.
3. Cherie Burns, *Step-Motherhood* (New York: Times Books, Random House, 1985), 215.

Chapter thirteen

1. William J. Bennett, *Human Events* (January 31, 1987), 100.
2. Ibid., 101.
3. Ruby Friesen, "What About Morality?" Beaverton Family Counseling Center *Counselgram* (Winter 1988).
4. Harry Munsinger, *Fundamentals of Child Development*, 2d ed. (San Diego: Holt, Rinehart, and Winston, 1971), 448.
5. Ibid., 448.
6. Ibid.
7. Andrew Murray, *The Children for Christ* (Chicago: Moody Press, 1952), 110.
8. Ibid., 67.